CW01424725

OUT OF THIS WORLD

West Midland Poems

Edited by Lisa Adlam

First published in Great Britain in 2015 by:

Young**Writers**

Remus House
Coltsfoot Drive
Peterborough
PE2 9BF
Telephone: 01733 890066
Website: www.youngwriters.co.uk

All Rights Reserved
Book Design by Ashley Janson
© Copyright Contributors 2015
SB ISBN 978-1-78443-571-4

Printed and bound in the UK by BookPrintingUK
Website: www.bookprintinguk.com

FOREWORD

Here at Young Writers our defining aim is to promote
the joys of reading and writing to children and
young adults and we are committed to nurturing the
creative talents of the next generation. By allowing
them to see their own work in print we believe their
confidence and love of creative writing will grow.

Out Of This World is our latest fantastic competition,
specifically designed to encourage the writing skills of
primary school children through the medium of poetry.
From the high quality of entries received, it is clear that
it really captured the imagination of all involved.

We are proud to present the resulting collection of
poems that we are sure will amuse and inspire.

An absorbing insight into the imagination and thoughts
of the young, we hope you will agree that this fantastic
anthology is one to delight the whole family again and again.

CONTENTS

Greenways Primary School, Stoke-On-Trent

Hillmorton Primary School, Rugby

John Shelton Primary School, Coventry

Johnstown Junior School, Wrexham

Jubilee Academy Mossley, Walsall

Manor Hill First School, Stone

Perry Beeches Infant School, Birmingham

Priory School, Birmingham

SS Peter & Paul Catholic Primary School, Lichfield

St Andrew's CE Primary School, Shrewsbury

St Francis Xavier Catholic Primary School, Oldbury

St Michael's CE Primary School, Birmingham

THE POEMS

Instructions For Living In Space

Step 1: See the gazillion bazillion stars in the blanket of darkness
Step 2: Smell the flames of the sun like rum making me giddy
Step 3: Taste the fruity raspberry flavour in the swirling gases all around
Step 4: Hear the ghostly magical whistling sounds, so beautiful
Step 5: Touch the colourful buttons and take a blast-off, 5, 4, 3, 2, 1!

Emma Hudson (8)

Once There Was An Alien Born . . .

Once there was an alien born
And she had one great horn
She had one round eye and liked to fly
She lived in a flower hole
I really think she was a mole
That very moment then
She jumped right out of her hole
And when she saw the bright light
It was quite a sight
She fell asleep and started to weep
Suddenly she woke up on a planet called Earth
She gave birth to a baby called Sirth
He grew up having no sight of his mother
And that was the end of the other alien
Sadly the alien started to get as red as a pepper
And that was the end
Because he started to bend.

Aisha Bibi (9)
Adderley Primary School, Birmingham

Planet Milky Way

On Planet Milky Way there lives somebody called Samantha Hop.
She likes to dress up and hop.
She is also very cheeky and likes to drink fizzy pop.
Oh my, she lives on a planet with only her family
But she dances all day very happily.

She is as pretty as a flower
And has a magical power.
Samantha goes to school
But in maths she dozes off and drools.
One night she was sleeping with her hand in her mouth
And remembered she lived on the south of Planet Milky Way.
In the morning for breakfast she ate hay.

Kaniz Ahmed (9)
Adderley Primary School, Birmingham

The Man On The Moon

He's alone on the moon
He's been called a loon
It's been said he has the eyes of the devil
He has even been called Nevil
But that's not his name
He's not insane
Abused and left out
People would always shout
Once a hero
Now he's zero
Left to die
Every night he would cry
Why am I here?
Left in fear

The man on the moon . . .

Jennifer Weston
Corngreaves Primary School, Cradley Heath

It's So Out Of This World!

The sun is a great ball of gas,
That is way bigger than anyone's mass.

Mercury is closest to the sun,
Cos Mercury is number one.

Venus is so not cold,
And doesn't contain any mould.

Earth is where we live and stay,
And we're never gonna leave here, hip, hip hooray!

Mars is where sandstorms appear,
And royal guardians carry spears.

Jupiter is the largest planet,
I hope no one ever bans it.

Saturn has a big round ring,
Which always makes me want to sing.

Uranus is a bluish green,
And is a planet almost everyone's seen.

Neptune is really blue,
And I assume it has aliens made of goo.

The moon is filled with craters,
Even ask those astronomical raters.

The Milky Way is where we're going today,
It's a black hole,
Oh no, that will rip out my soul . . .

It's so out of this *world* . . .

Quinton Ikediashi (10)
Corngreaves Primary School, Cradley Heath

Out Into Space

If I could travel to the moon,
I would realise only so soon.
But if I appear to the future
I would transport to Jupiter.

As I walk through a portal to Mars,
I wonder if I will see the stars.
As I jump onto the Milky Way
It seems like everything has faded away.

I would have a race,
To appear in space.
I would fly a rocket
At such a pace.
But I wouldn't forget
To tie my lace.

Iram Shahzad
Corngreaves Primary School, Cradley Heath

Stars

You twinkle and twinkle throughout the night,
When darkness falls you give me light.
As we gaze upon your wonderful shine
I seem to know that everything is fine.

As you shout goodnight
With all of your might,
I could come and watch you shine if I could fly
Because you are the brightest star in the sky.

Paris Hunt (10)
Corngreaves Primary School, Cradley Heath

The Trip To Space

Space, space, ever so high
Is it above or under the sky?
Lies, lies, I'm fed up of lies
What is actually above the dark blue sky?
Time to see what is there
Could it be a dream
Or a real-life nightmare?

Jamie Mole
Corngreaves Primary School, Cradley Heath

Rocket

R oland is an alien who
O verwhelms astronauts
C ally his wife is so nice
K alum, their son has run away
E veryone tries to find him
T ogether we will find him, Roland and Cally says.

Erin May Callahan (11)
Corngreaves Primary School, Cradley Heath

The Rocket Race

Slowly start to build up pace
We're off on our journey to space
Look to your left, see the stars
Where will we end up?
Jupiter or Mars?

Danreiko Henry (11)
Corngreaves Primary School, Cradley Heath

Mars

The fourth planet from the sun,
Is freezing cold and icy,
It's frosty, bitter, perishing, chilly,
No, not the chilli, that's spicy.

There's a mountain,
No, it's roaring,
It's a volcano,
But no lava is spurting and pouring.

Down here it's pitch black,
In this huge canyon thing,
Dark, gloomy, murky, shadowy,
It's really dingy and dim.

Down a tunnel like a mouse I crept,
I took out a torch in my pocket I kept,
There was a Martian that soundly slept,
So away with my torch I ran and leapt.

The rose red sand,
The ruby red sky,
The crimson red craters
Are amazing, my oh my.

Now it's time to set up the village,
With pressurised houses and walls,
With entertainment like cinemas
And bats, rackets and balls.

Mars is desolate,
Apart from the stars,
That twinkle down like the friendliest friends
Of Mars.

What's that rock ball?
Rocky and hard,
Oh it's a moon I thought,
But I stepped on a jagged rock shard.

As I examined the blood on my foot
(I was in my pressurised room)
I decided it was serious
Then saw the other moon.

This one was much the same,
Apart from it was prettier,
Whereas the other one was dirtier
And grittier.

Boooooosssh!
Was that a cannon ball?
Nope, it was a meteorite,
That evilly decided to fall.

Outside again
I plant my flag,
Mars is England's now
And the flag doesn't sag.

Barney Doel (10)
Deanery CE Primary School, Sutton Coldfield

Great Mars

G ravity on Mars is like you are a superhero
R ed grime blanketing Mars' surface
E nergised astronauts to jump onto the rocky Mars
A s red as a juicy tomato
T remendous terrifying wind howling like a wolf

M agnificent Mars frozen up in the sky
A stonishing sound of the sand swirling around the rocket
R apidly breathing astronauts shocked by the Mars' atmosphere
S trong horrific sand storms.

Cian Fox (9)
Deanery CE Primary School, Sutton Coldfield

Walking On Mars

Standing strongly on the edge of Mars,
All I hear is the whistling wind
Blowing across the red dusty surface.

Immediately I hear volcanoes exploding
Like shooting stars flying across the sky.

Inside I feel butterflies in my tummy,
Then I glance around to see
Shimmering stars over the universe.

Finally I find the menacing volcanoes
Right in front of my eyes.

Then the volcanoes explode
With their fantastic lava spitting across the land,
Suddenly I feel the sand rush past
Like a hurricane.

Then I fly back to Earth
After exploring the fascinating Mars.

Tilly Mae Slowley (10)
Deanery CE Primary School, Sutton Coldfield

Mars

Standing sturdily on the dusty surface of Mars,
Looking up at comforting twin moons and dazzling twinkling stars.
In the distance a ferocious volcano juts up and is spitting lava at me,
Sharp rocks are blood-piercing daggers pointing viciously,
Red sand violently charging and chasing me around
Till it calmly, gently settles on the ground.
Emptiness echoes like a spooky silent room.
Mars, I've made it.

Harriet Martin (9)
Deanery CE Primary School, Sutton Coldfield

Monstrous Mission To Mars

Eyes closed,
Daring to peek,
Starlit sky surrounded me,
Opening wider, straining my eyes
I began to see the unmistakable figure
Of Olympus Mons standing proudly in vast emptiness,
Heavy breathing filled my clear fish bowl,
Like water rising,
I knew it was time,
Shaking violently, my sweaty hands
Wrestled with the steel door.
It clicked open . . .

Red dust floated magically around me
Like Christmas lights above my head,
Here I was, standing proudly
On the graceful red tomato of outer space.

Carefully avoiding the massive craters,
I wandered further into the history books.
Wide open my eyes darted gleefully
From left to right,
Taking in all that surrounded me,
I stood in awe.

Instantly the mood changed,
Super strong sand storms swirled swiftly around me.
Fear rose inside as the temperature dropped.
Nothing prepared me for the sub-zero temperature,
Attacking my body viciously and aggressively.

Wild winds whistled continuously,
Producing a high-pitched shriek
That filled my thoughts,
However . . .
History was made.

Cameron Jack (9), Dena Shiltagh (10) & Lewis
Deanery CE Primary School, Sutton Coldfield

Mars

Standing strongly on the ground,
Booting a mound,
I was a feather on the surface of Mars
Then climbed into a car,
As I turned the key, the engine screeched!

I heard mumbling of rocks,
As I heard my socks quiver,
I clambered out of the old, battered buggy
I stood there on the ice
That roared beneath mc!

I thought at first I was as afraid as a mouse
As the ice screamed, I thought I'd bounce
As I went in, the ice became jelly
And as wide as a country
I couldn't swim as I could hear deafening death
Was this the end?

I smelt the grains of dust
I swam up like a fish, I must
As I got out I smelt the smoke of a volcano
Spitting out lava, around me I saw the daggers of rocks big, small
I was surrounded by dust storms
I had nowhere to go!

I saw the twin moons looking down on me
With big beaming smiles
It was like they knew what I felt like
I heard dreading death coming nearer
Nearer, nearer and nearer, argh!
What if it's my imagination?

Fraser Burns (10)
Deanery CE Primary School, Sutton Coldfield

Mission To Mars

Sands whispering,
Air whistling,
As I move I feel
A slight mixture
Of anxiety and excitement.

A gentle sandstorm
Rushes to my feet.
As if a small crowd
Wants to meet me.

I breathe heavily
Inside my mask.
12 o'clock strikes
As I cautiously dodge
The final black crater.

I whisper to myself
A sigh of relief.
As I finally reach the point
To plant my flag,
I feel like a lion
Standing proud above the jungle.

I place the flag
And make one final voyage
Through Mars' beautiful landscape.

I make my way
Through the craters . . .
And then *crack!*
Argh!

Jack Bower (10)
Deanery CE Primary School, Sutton Coldfield

Out Of This World – Mars

Mars is like a squashed tomato,
Being bullied by asteroids,
Dusty dunes, desolate deserts
And two moons!

A sea of black emptiness surrounds it,
Low temperatures,
As cold as Antarctica,
Deserts like the Sahara,
Drifting through space like a balloon,
In 2025 people will be living there soon!

The dust stealthily creeps up your spacesuit,
Winds howling at you,
50 miles per hour,
It is as cold as an ice shower!

You can see it tiptoe around the sun,
Like a robber stealing precious jewels,
Olympus Mons (a volcano) sits proudly in vast emptiness.

Not a single drop of water,
Or food,
Mars is not good for survival,
Especially arrival,
So it could suffocate you in coldness,
Or wipe you away in a sandstorm,
-187 degrees,
You will die,
Or freeze . . .

Cian Burke (9)
Deanery CE Primary School, Sutton Coldfield

Beautiful Mars

Leaping down steadily, I gaze around
This extraordinary planet I can see
Red rocks in all shapes and sizes
The floor is full of them.

As I look up I see no sky
But a beautiful blackness
And in that blackness are 10,000 bright stars
Smiling at me, the red dust seems to float up and down
As if I am in a sea.

I can feel the soft sand brush against my legs,
I feel the light of 10,000 stars shining on me!
I sit on the smooth yet sharp rocks, to take it all in.

While I sit there, I begin to think
Could I live here?
On this rose red planet?
No! It couldn't be done, could it?

I breathe in heavily trying to get a whiff of Mars,
But I feel very upset when instead of smelling Mars,
I smell my horrid spacesuit,
It smells like plastic and rubber, urgh!

I feel so alive here on Mars
Staring into space with a smile on my face,
As I wonder over to the rocket across the blood red floor,
I give a wave to Mars,
For I will see it once more!

Cydney Riley-Blackwood
Deanery CE Primary School, Sutton Coldfield

Misty, Marvellous Mars

Pacing on Mars,
It is a blank red apple,
Dancing in space,
A beautiful place!

It is like a freezer,
Blowing in your face,
Or a fan,
Wherever you go,
It follows you.

Listen to the whistling wind,
Touch the soft sand,
Stare at the starlit sky,
Place your hand on the flag.

Tiptoeing, very quietly around,
Searching,
Mountains, far in the distance, I can see,
Sand dunes, for miles, are what I can make out,
A beautiful place.

It is like a danger zone,
With sand storms punching upon face,
And the mass is mist,
You always get lost,
Now you think,
It's a horrible place.

Harry Davies (9)
Deanery CE Primary School, Sutton Coldfield

My First Step On Mars

I stood and looked at the white shiny rocket door.
As I slowly turned the rusty black handle.
My nerves and excitement grew.
There before me.
Dusty and mysterious, a bright bouncy ball lay.
My eyes lit up like a glowing light bulb.
It was absolutely beautiful!
I put my foot down onto the rough, red surface
Of the wonderful floating marble.

A smile grew on my small face,
As a monstrous storm rushed past the bottom of my heavy spacesuit.
Amazed I looked up to the glistening starlit sky.
I had an extraordinary wander round
The top of the planet,
It was as cold as a freezer
But it was totally worth it.
I loved the little pot holes,
There were big ones and small ones.
I nearly stood in one by my mistake.
I kept thinking, *wow!*
I'm the first woman to stand on Mars.

Renée Scadeng (9)
Deanery CE Primary School, Sutton Coldfield

Mars

Standing sturdily on the rose red surface of Mars,
Immediately, soft silence struck me like a scorching flash of light.
The dust swirled round Mars like a sand storm.
Mars running round the solar system as I spoke,
Stars looking down at me like each light of the world
Had flown up and landed in space.
Rough rocks standing in my way,
Looking round, being pushed and pulled left, right, left, right
Because of the whirling, whistling wind.
Red dust flying around me.
Suddenly I saw the sand chasing me to the volcano,
Volcanoes spitting and spurting out lava like a fountain,
Finally reaching the middle of Mars,
Celebrating.
Engulfed in sand,
Sharp rocks were daggers.
Carrying on till the top of Mars.
Shivering as the temperature got below -20 degrees.
Two moons smiled down at me
Comforting me each step of the way,
Twin moons looking at me.

Jessica Plimmer (9)
Deanery CE Primary School, Sutton Coldfield

My Experience On Mars

As I landed on the surface of Mars
I saw some very shimmering stars.
Walking on Mars was eerie and chilling,
But exploring the planet was ever so willing.
Dust storms and volcanoes are what I heard,
But no sound of a songbird.

As I walked on many minutes later,
I nearly fell into a crater.
Then I walked around the hole that was deep
And I climbed up some mountains
Which were enormously steep.

Then I strolled onto the ice cap of Mars
Which could freeze the engines out of cars.
The temperature was minus 55 degrees,
And the ice was as slippery as a bucket of grease.

I feel quite sad that I have to go,
Leaving all the things that I don't know.
The moon came at night to shine,
I can't wait to go to the planet that's mine!

Daniel James Hewett (9)
Deanery CE Primary School, Sutton Coldfield

Mission To Mars

Standing strongly on the rose red surface of Mars,
Immediately hush struck me like a scorching light.
On the horizon, a volcano jutted up and was spitting out lava like a cobra.
Sand charged towards me, churning viciously around and pulling me into it,
Pointed rocks were daggers piercing through, surrounding me like a building.
Twin moons smiled at me, comfortingly dozing into sunrise,
As I walked forward I saw the red dust scattering the floor.

Samuel Windridge (10)
Deanery CE Primary School, Sutton Coldfield

The Red Planet

Sitting comfy on the warm seat
With hands waving side to side in the window
Soon blasting off to spectacular space
But who's going to win the space race?
Countdown has begun
Now who's the first man on Mars?

Being guided through the starlit sky
Dodging the changing asteroids
Waving past the moon
On an epic journey.

Soon approaching the deserted planet,
Heart pounding moments.

Sand brushing in the air
Getting my flag and pushing it in the ground
Rumble, rumble, rumble,
I hear
Then out of nowhere
A sandstorm, *boom!*
Wait, I wake up in my head!

Micah Thomas (9)
Deanery CE Primary School, Sutton Coldfield

Mission To Mars

Looking at the rocks like they're monstrous mountains,
As stars stare at you, like you're having a staring contest.
Immediately, you think rocks are running around you,
Trying to trip you over.
You feel sand hitting you every second,
Shooting through the cracks of your silky spacesuit.
You smell sizzling, scorching red-hot ash,
Being spat out from a volcano,
Thinking it's a fire-breathing dragon and an ash spitting cobra,
When you walk it's like you're the first person to walk the Earth.

Calum Dubb (9)
Deanery CE Primary School, Sutton Coldfield

Landing On Mars

Standing strongly on the rose red surface of Mars,
Immediately, silence struck me like a scorching light.
On the horizon, a volcano jutted up and was spitting out lava like a cobra.
Sand, charging towards me, swirling viciously around and spiralling me.
Sharp rocks were daggers piercing their way through,
Surrounding me like a building.
Twin moons smiled at me comfortingly, dozing into sunrise.
Emptiness echoed with the scary sound of silence,
My heart thumping, trying to pull itself out of my chest.

That was it, just that.
No more was to be heard.
What else could I come across?
Not lots.
Shadows creeping up behind me,
What could it be?
The spacecraft waiting for me,
I was ready, let's go.

Charlotte King (10)
Deanery CE Primary School, Sutton Coldfield

Monstrous Mission To Mars!

Spooky shifting sands never stay still
Freezing winds whisper around my toes.
A long decade stands behind me as I take my first step.
Looking up I see bright shining stars, blinding me.
In my helmet all I hear is me,
Breathing like a croaking frog.

I am worried for my children,
But happy at the same time.
One thing that I hope my children do is be pioneers.
Can you believe I am standing on Mars?

Ellie-May Stokes (10)
Deanery CE Primary School, Sutton Coldfield

19

Amazing Mars

Mars floats in space like a red balloon,
Mars is a misty desert of coldness,
I watch it loop the loop around the boiling hot sun,
It is so fun,
The sand stealthily creeps up your gigantic space pants.

Nasty asteroids bully Mars,
They create crazy craters,
Asteroids are a scorching hot ball of fire,
Mars is a bright red battered tomato.

I silently tiptoe towards the starlit sky,
And it doesn't say bye,
It looks hot,
But it's not,
It's around -110°c
You'll probably freeze.

Olympus Mons sits proudly in vast emptiness,
I wish I could go in an enormous rocket up, up and away,
And land on Mars and say hip hip hooray!

William John Nutt (10)
Deanery CE Primary School, Sutton Coldfield

Monstrous Mission To Mars!

Sandy sand storms race towards the ginormous aircraft,
Which has colourful stripes dancing on its surface.
Beautiful blackness fills the sky,
And stars smile from way up high.

Mars is a bright red balloon doing the loop the loop
Round the spherical sun,
Passing the Olympus Mons,
Standing proudly in the vast emptiness.
Mars is like a battered tomato
Tiptoeing towards the starlit sky, ready for bed.

Lydia Donohoe (9)
Deanery CE Primary School, Sutton Coldfield

Alone On Mars

Standing still in a rose red gloom,
Dust blocking my sight.
Twirling, whirling on the wind,
Sand whistled between my toes.

Trying to walk, feet sinking in the soft, warm surface.
Emerging in the distance a mountain
Of red volcanoes became visible through shadows.

Stars smiled down from the dark sky.
Twin moons shimmered and gleamed
In the thin atmosphere.

Me and Mars, running around the solar system,
In our own orbit around the sun.

My heart was as delicate as a rose petal
Looking in the cold, breezy, bitter sky
Seeing all the twinkling stars shining
In the hazy red sky, fading away.

Emily Jack
Deanery CE Primary School, Sutton Coldfield

Great Big Mars

G ravity on Mars is freedom,
R ed as monstrous lava,
E xhilarating to step on that dusty surface,
A s red as a tomato,
T he dust blankets the red surface,

B ellowing deep down in the craters,
I ce cold frost temperatures,
G iant holes in the ground everywhere,

M ars is a battered tomato,
A rmoured like a knight,
R aging redness staring at you,
S trong strapping sand storms!

Matthew Licari (10)
Deanery CE Primary School, Sutton Coldfield

Magnificent Mars

M agnificent Mars tiptoes slowly across the globe
A stronauts flying furiously across the battered tomato
G reat craters forming a troop
N atural and brilliant men walking on Mars
I t is a great achievement to get to Mars
F abulous astronauts floating on Mars
I njuries have happened because of the rocket going at the
speed of light
C hildren are watching the first few steps on Mars
E xcitement is all over Earth because the first man, Bob,
stood on Mars.
N ight sky as dark as black ink
T orrential sand storms going millions of miles

M en are packing up to go home
A re they ready to go back home?
R oaring to go home the astronauts are ready
S trange things happen as they go back down to Earth.

Tom Lockrey (9)
Deanery CE Primary School, Sutton Coldfield

Men On Mars!

Staring out of the compact shuttle,
I spotted our destination,
A giant red tomato lying among the gleeful stars,
In a blanket of emptiness.

Nervously I stepped out,
Onto the great freezer!
Carefully avoiding the scattered rocks,
Staring annoyingly up at me.

Sand and dust immediately swam around me,
Attacking me viciously like a tiger!
I was forced to close my eyes,
As angry rocks bounced off my fish tank!

Hannah Simpson (10)
Deanery CE Primary School, Sutton Coldfield

The Red Planet

Standing sturdily on the dust-covered surface of Mars,
Silence suddenly strikes me like a scorching light.
On the horizon, a volcano juts up and is spitting lava like a vicious cobra.
Sand chases the slow wind and swirls around me,
Sharp rocks are daggers piercing my boots.
Twin moons smile at me dozing into sunrise,
It's an extraordinary feeling, bouncing past craters,
Soil oozing in my toes.
Stars twinkle like thousands of lanterns floating through space,
Somewhere, in the blackness Earth bobs around turning from day to night.
The rusted iron boils red at my feet,
Craters dip like mole hills dipping and curving at the sides.
Crumbling by my shoes the red pebbles crunch,
Just like the parkway path from home.
Mars floating around the sun as we go.

Jenna Harries (10)
Deanery CE Primary School, Sutton Coldfield

Misty Mars

M agical Mars howls with the wind. Eerie, right?
 I n with a chance of most mysterious planet of all time.
S ightings of a masterpiece, it is cool!
T ime taking gusts of sand hurtling and falling upon Mars at great speeds.
Y oung and fit, but don't let that fool you. Its nickname is the Devil's eye.

M isty Mars with dust dashing across it, oh great sand
A mazing mountains like Olympus Mons make Mars look prettier by the second.
R ushing, racing sand/dust literally flies across the red planet.
S ilence falls upon the bruised tomato, Mars, it brings out the Devil's eye.

Jack Owen (9)
Deanery CE Primary School, Sutton Coldfield

Mars

Mars . . .
Is a red battered tomato,
Stars smiling down on me,
There is silence,
Mars,
A cold misty planet,
Sandy sandstorms everywhere,
Mars,
Is as cold as a freezer,
The wind is whistling,
Sand rustling in the distance,
Not to mention the red sandy dust floating by,
And beautiful blackness,
Mars,
Silently tiptoes towards the moonlit sky,
I can see gigantic craters everywhere,
I now know the monstrous mission to Mars has begun!

Megan Harrison (9)
Deanery CE Primary School, Sutton Coldfield

The Red Planet

T he mission to Mars travelling in a rocket,
H ope that it doesn't pull a socket.
E xtraterrestrials waiting up there,

R ound heads with an evil stare.
E quipped with fish bowl helmets and oxygen tanks,
D aring astronauts want to warn their ranks.

P etrified people bubbling inside,
L anding makes them want to hide.
A dults they may be but,
N ASA doesn't know they want Mummy.
E veryone watching in awe,
T wo astronauts on that big red tomato, Mars.

Morgan Longmore (10)
Deanery CE Primary School, Sutton Coldfield

Mission To Mars

Starting strongly with the roots of my feet stuck firmly into the ground
The lovely twinkling stars shone on me.
Moments later I looked up and saw the horizon,
The mountains they were like the most beautiful women I had ever seen.
All I heard five minutes later was the stamping sound of the rough hard rocks
Dancing around me, I felt like me and this dazzling planet were hiding
Away from the gleaming sun,
When all the sun wanted to do was play with us.
Through the shadows a volcano emerged from the red rose surface of Mars
It was the most frightening thing I had ever witnessed.
The volcano was like a cobra spitting venom,
However the volcano was spitting lava instead.
The last thing I saw were two brilliant moons flying around me.

Malakai Florey-Meah (10)
Deanery CE Primary School, Sutton Coldfield

Mars

Standing strongly on the red rose surface of Mars,
A smell of nervous sweat filling my spacesuit.
The dust is swirling around me like a sandstorm,
It feels like I'm flying!
Rocks are cartwheeling around me like lost puppies.

I look across the horizon and see a volcano,
Rising up and spitting out lava.
Then I look up into the pitch-black sky
And the sparkling stars and magnificent moons are looking down
Comforting me in every way.

I can see the stars,
I think I am the first person on Mars.

Sophia Baxter (10)
Deanery CE Primary School, Sutton Coldfield

Mars

As I step ever closer, the smell of chips is gone,
And now there is no smell at all,
I'm walking with no gravity,
My face is amazed as I shiver,
The temperature is as cold as a freezer.

I look up and see stars smiling happily at me,
I'm now on a battered tomato,
I don't mind my smell because I'm packed in this chunky suit,
As I walk, the craters are as deep as a double decker bus tilted down,
I feel the wind howling around me,
As I walk on the rough surface, asteroids are bullying the juicy red planet.

Day and night changes in seconds,
Wind and storms change in seconds,
Attacking my heart, leaving my friends and family at home.

Adam Parr (10)
Deanery CE Primary School, Sutton Coldfield

Magical Mars

As I took my first step onto the orange sea,
Crimson dust swirling around was all I could see.
As a little boy I lay in bed,
While visions of Mars danced in my head.
Now I was looking through the clear goldfish bowl,
With stars smiling down on me.

Where bullying asteroids had created huge craters,
Hopping around impatiently, I waited 'til later
When my mates would come.
I rested on a rock and started to hum
And suddenly, a great gust of wind whistled past,
Knocking over my waiter.

Erin Baker (9)
Deanery CE Primary School, Sutton Coldfield

Mars

Standing still in a rose red gloom,
Dust blocking my sight.
Twirling, whirling on the wind, sand
Whistled between my boots.

Trying to walk, feet sinking in the soft surface,
Emerging in the distance a mountain of red volcanoes
Became visible through the shadows,
Stars smiled down from the dark sky.

Twin moons shimmered and gleamed in,
The thin atmosphere.
Me and Mars, running around the solar system
In our own orbit around the sun.

The ground was as cold as an ice rink,
On the freezing land.
I'd got a cold night up ahead.

Finlay John Hardcastle (9)
Deanery CE Primary School, Sutton Coldfield

Mars

M ars
 I s a gigantic spherical desert,
S uper storms walk over,
S lightly rough to touch,
 I nteresting and powerful,
O xygen outstandingly low,
N o life.

T here's silence,
O ut in the galaxy far away.

M ars is a sandy creation,
A s the stars smile upon,
R ed planet glimmers,
S o don't go near or you'll freeze like ice.

Daisy Jessica Horton Delicate (10)
Deanery CE Primary School, Sutton Coldfield

Man Standing On Mars

I was standing on Mars.
The Earth was in sight.
The surface was bumpy.
The stars were gleaming bright.

The surface was as hard as red diamonds.
The red dust was twinkling on my feet.
It was as silent as an abandoned desert.
Help me!

Emerging in the distance
There was a massive volcano.
Lava as hot as the gleaming sun.
Stars were smiling down,
Lighting the surface of Mars.

Petrified of loneliness,
Abandoned on a foreign planet forever!

Frederick Thomas Perks (10)
Deanery CE Primary School, Sutton Coldfield

Mission To Mars

M onstrous mission to Mars,
 I started the engine and blasted off. Off I went blasting into space.
S itting comfy on the seat, hands on window, looking out.
S hooting across the universe I dreamt about Mars.
 I approached the mighty Mars (as strong as a Roman).
O lympus Mons sitting proudly in the vast emptiness.
N obody there except for me and the smiling stars.

T ornadoes sucking me up. Trying to stay on my feet.
O pen space all around me, all I was thinking was, *which way to go?*

M ars as cold as a freezer, where to go for heat?
A s red as a tomato.
R ockets blasting off at the speed of light back to Earth.
S uper adventure.

Emily Scott (9)
Deanery CE Primary School, Sutton Coldfield

Mission To Mars

The red rose planet was as cold as can be,
It was like the air was trying to kill me.
Landing on my feet I heard the whistling wind,
Blowing in my hair powerfully.
The sand rushed straight past me like a hurricane.
Immediately I went to the volcano with red hot lava,
It was the best thing I had ever seen,
It was the best place I had ever been.
But I was really sad because I was missing my friend,
While I was turning round this bend.
Then I walked to the top of the planet,
With my pet bunny rabbit.
Then my friend landed on Mars
And she bought some toy cars.
Then I showed her my board game
And she took her first aim.

Ellen Austin (9)
Deanery CE Primary School, Sutton Coldfield

Mysterious Mars

M y hands shake fearfully,
Y anking the door into the unknown,
S natching my only chance to be the first person,
T o step foot and hear the howling sounds of Mars.
E verything is dusty, I taste a sand storm,
R acing past my feet . . .
I am standing on a big battered tomato,
O ut there on Earth I see my child,
U nder me wishing, hoping I am there.
S teadily I examine a rock, it looks like my son's face.

M ars is just like a big frozen blob of red play dough.
A t the top of a mountain called Olympus Mons, I
R ace around in my Mars buggy,
S tuffing samples in my bag to examine later.

Luke Windsor-Trappett (9)
Deanery CE Primary School, Sutton Coldfield

Mission To Mars

Lowering off the rocket, is the flag in my pocket?
Getting closer and closer to massive Mars
Looking around, where to put my flag on the ground
The twin moons grinning down on me.

A vicious volcano spitting smoke like a king cobra
The volcano literally is a beast, he is roaring like a lion
Digesting boiling molten lava as hot as the sun.
Rapid rocks running throughout the land of dust
Trying to trip you over!
An army of rocks trooping together to block me going on.

Standing strong on the rocky surface of Mars
A gleaming light hits me like a bullet
Remembering the person who inspired me, Neil Armstrong
And now look at me, first human on Mars
I will always be remembered.

Ethan Wall (10)
Deanery CE Primary School, Sutton Coldfield

Monstrous Mission To Mars

Creepily creeping out of the shiny spacecraft,
The astronaut trod onto the extraordinary planet, Mars,
While slowly bouncing into the calm air.

He looked around at the glittery stars staring down at him,
Thinking intensely of what he'd left behind.
Emotionally holding his heart,
And breathing into his fish tank helmet.

Kicking the sand and catching it in his hand,
Jumping and bouncing with no gravity.

I remember my home . . .
Standing on a battered tomato.

Casee Burton (9)
Deanery CE Primary School, Sutton Coldfield

Mission To Mars

When I was up in space on Mars
I was thinking about the chocolate bars
Looking at the empty space
In a dream I thought I was up in space.
I wish I was up in Mars
Creating community, a cinema and most of all, a restaurant.

I am finally here on Mars
My dream has come true
It's a lonely red planet
It's very, very silent Mars is.

It's a beautiful red planet
Silent as can be
I wish I could go again.

Bye-bye Mars, see you soon!

Bethany Donna Andrea Kay (10)
Deanery CE Primary School, Sutton Coldfield

Magical Mars

As I enter the red planet Mars,
All I see is the everlasting sparkling red surface,

The surface blowing everywhere,
Although it is very cold,

As I see asteroids as big as aeroplanes,
One I manage to avoid,
But others hit me,
I get knocked to the ground,
But I still go and wander around,
Even though it's a bit cold.

When I leave I'll have forever memories,
Of the wind that howls like a dog!
Magical Mars is a red fiery tomato and a floating desert,
But with a red surface!

Kate Dandy (9)
Deanery CE Primary School, Sutton Coldfield

Travel To Space

Standing strongly on the red dust, as I quickly glanced across the incredible Mars,
All I could hear was the shimmering dust whistling between my toes,
Volcanoes were deafening, gushing out lava,
Suddenly it was silent, volcanoes, mini hills, were slumped there on the dusty ground.
Mars is phenomenal, I could see the super solar system, I wished I could stay.
When I looked up it was like thousands and thousands of shimmering smiley stars
Were looking down on me.
I had butterflies in my tummy, nervous and excited at the same time!
Would you like to go to Mars?
I sadly got back on my rocket and went back to Earth,
I still remember that day!

Lauren Lus (10)
Deanery CE Primary School, Sutton Coldfield

Mission To Mars

M ars is a battered tomato.
I   put my helmet on and my suit.
S tanding by the door (here goes)
S tepping on the red planet I slowly walked up and down
I couldn't hear anything or see anything
O nly walking by myself, I can't see anything
N othing, I can't see my rocket, I think I have searched everywhere.

T rying, yes still trying to look for it.
O nly myself still looking for it.

M arvellous I eventually find my rocket, I think it is time to go.
A nd eventually I am near the door of my rocket.
R ocket, yes my rocket is going to blast off. 5, 4, 3, 2, 1.
S itting in my rocket staring out of my window, looking at the stars
   I see Earth. Nearly there, I am there!

Fenton William Sleigh (9)
Deanery CE Primary School, Sutton Coldfield

Planets Of The Universe

Standing strongly on the rose red burning surface of Mars,
Immediately silence struck me like a scorching beam.

On the horizon a volcano jutted up and was spitting out lava like a
cobra.
The sand engulfed me viciously and was pulling me hard.
Sharp rocks were daggers piercing through,
Surrounding me like a building closing in on me.

Twin moons smiled at me comfortingly, dozing into sunrise.
As I took one step I felt a lot of power come to me
As I planted the USA flag.

I've done it!

Rohan Chana (9)
Deanery CE Primary School, Sutton Coldfield

The Red One

Standing strongly on the rose red surface of Mars,
Immediately silence strikes me like a scorching light.
On the horizon, a volcano juts up and is spitting out scalding lava like
a cobra.
Sand charges towards me, churning viciously around and tows me
in.
Pointed rocks are daggers piercing through, they encircle me like a
building.
Twin moons beam at me comfortingly dozing into sunrise;
Emptiness echoes with the spine-chilling soundless atmosphere,
My heart thumping, trying to pull out of my chest,
I've done it.

Zack Mansell (9)
Deanery CE Primary School, Sutton Coldfield

Mars

Standing on the fourth planet,
In the freezing, chilly coldness.
Standing in the distance of the horizon
I had the slightest sweat
Falling down my spacesuit.

I could see mountains, moons and more,
Even volcanoes roaring and snoring.

The red rocky dust surroundings in the air,
At first I didn't care,
At last I got there
And when I got there I loved it.

Oliver Barber (10)
Deanery CE Primary School, Sutton Coldfield

Mission To Mars

Standing strongly on the rose red dust of Mars,
You could hear the very faint whistle of the wind.
And you could spot thousands of shimmering stars.
The rocks in the air were like rhinos charging at you.
In the distance there were ginormous craters,
They were like pot holes.
You could already feel the bitter cold from inside the rocket.
On the horizon a volcano emerged
And spat lava out like a fountain.
Finally I made it back to family and friends.

Jack Horton (9)
Deanery CE Primary School, Sutton Coldfield

Mission To Mars

Standing strongly on the rocky-red dust of Mars,
I could see the stars smiling and the moon glittering on me.
In the distance I could hear a penetrating noise of volcanoes
exploding.
I could see Mars running round the solar system,
And red dust whistled gently up my toes.
I could see sharp rocks which were like daggers
And mountains running round Mars.

Josh Stapleton (10)
Deanery CE Primary School, Sutton Coldfield

Spacemen

Spacemen wear spacesuits,
With space boots.
They have telescopes that zoom,
They sometimes see asteroids that go boom,
They see comets,
They see planets,
They travel around in rockets,
The sun is very hot,
Do you think it's not?

Thomas Haynes (7)
Greenacres Primary School, Shrewsbury

Space

Zooming past the galaxy,
Space boots like rockets,
Exploring mysterious planets,
Intelligent life seeing comets,
Time travel and dimensions,
Stars are bright as the moon,
The world, so big.

Samuel Heath (7)
Greenacres Primary School, Shrewsbury

The Moon

The moon,
Comes up at night,
That is what makes the moonlight,
I wonder how it does such a thing,
Maybe it just has to sing,
Or maybe not,
It might just have to make itself hot
And that is the moon.

Keira Austin (8)
Greenacres Primary School, Shrewsbury

Space

Space is big
Space is wide
And I think that I can have a ride
Planets are big
Some even have a wig
Space is a lot of space
There are lots of comets
And planets in space.

Kelsey Tina Fletcher (8)
Greenacres Primary School, Shrewsbury

Planet

P lanets are big
L ife is only on Earth
A liens still might live on Earth
N obody knows for definite
E xploring the universe is fun
T ime travelling is an adventure.

Luis Antony Jones (8)
Greenacres Primary School, Shrewsbury

Space!

S is for satellite spacesuit
P is for Planet Pluto
A is for adventure alien
C is for comet constellation
E is for exploring alien.

Austin Poole (7)
Greenacres Primary School, Shrewsbury

Space

S is for spectacular stars
P is for peculiar Pluto
A is for amazing aliens
C is for crazy constellations
E is for enormous Earth.

Molly Rowson (8)
Greenacres Primary School, Shrewsbury

Space

S is for spectacular space
P is for Pluto's planet
A is for amazing astronaut
C is for cool comet
E is for exploring existence.

Amber Griffiths (8)
Greenacres Primary School, Shrewsbury

The Spaceship

C is for comet constellation
R is for rockets
A is for awesome astronomy
S is for space continuum
H is for hurtling.

Ben Cumming (8)
Greenacres Primary School, Shrewsbury

Star

S is for space
T is for travelling through space
A is for aliens
R is for rocket.

Kian Grocott (7)
Greenacres Primary School, Shrewsbury

The Planets

I can see rockets whooshing into space,
I can see the space bat angel dragon singing as it flies,
The stars are shining like the sun,
What is space?
Space, space, space is dark.

I can hear the sound of rockets whooshing strong in space,
I can see stars shining in the dark sky,
Big asteroids are whooshing past me,
Space is ace,
In space the order of the planets is Mercury, Venus,
Earth, Mars, Jupiter, Saturn, Uranus, Neptune, Pluto.

Mars is red, it looks like a ball of dirt,
I can see a big planet glowing far away,
Rockets are blowing up as they come up to space.

Erin Moreton-Powell (7)
Greenways Primary School, Stoke-On-Trent

The Sun And Moon

The sun is shining bright with all its might.
Space is big and bright.
The moon is in sight.
The moon is high in the sky.

To get to the moon you need a rocket.
I have space stuff in my pocket.
I see a satellite dish,
Quick, make a wish.

It's a new texture, don't you see,
It does feel like it to me.
I see a flying saucer with an alien in it,
I don't think I could fit in it.

Flying rocks are whooshing past,
And rockets are flying fast.
There are craters in the moon
And the sun is burning hot.

If you put a flag on the moon,
Just remember it is not a spoon.
There is no gravity on the moon
But you can see your spoon.

Jemima Price (8)
Greenways Primary School, Stoke-On-Trent

The Epic Space

Rockets are whooshing every night,
The sun shines bright like some fire,
Astronauts' suits are white,
The sun is bright.

The sky is dark,
The moon is still in the black sky,
I can see lots of shiny stars,
The aliens are waiting for food on the moon!

Lewis Butler (8)
Greenways Primary School, Stoke-On-Trent

Relaxing In Space

Things are magic in space
Are you touching the glowing moon?
Space can be a peaceful thing.
Shooting stars coming quick,
Have you made your wish?
Shiny silver stars floating in the sky.

Rockets whooshing, whooping into space,
Wild, whooshing, shooting stars going all over the moon.
You're touching the bumpy moon,
You can see astronauts coming to you.
How does it feel in space?
The super, shiny, silver stars floating,
Can you see the sparklers of the magic?

Don't worry about no gravity, have fun!
I can see planets spinning,
What can you see?
No gravity is fine.
The half moon is smiling at you.

Hannah Hayes (8)
Greenways Primary School, Stoke-On-Trent

Earth

Rockets soaring into space
The space bat angel dragon is snoring in space,
There are stars, Saturn and astronauts,
Space is cool,
Astronauts floating like kangaroos,
I can see aliens waving at me,
I can see lights and Earth is like lights,
Earth is colourful,
I can see stars in the black sky
And the moon,
The stars are yellow.

Louis Ibinson (7)
Greenways Primary School, Stoke-On-Trent

Planets

Rockets whooshing in the air.
I can see the moon.
Aliens shooting past,
I can see the sun whooshing.
Darkness in the air.
Faster and faster go the planets.
Mars is having an alien invasion.
I can see planets everywhere.
I can feel the rocket blasting off.
I can see little bits of the moon falling of.
I can see aliens waving at me.
I can see glitter.
I can see the aliens' invasion.
I can see the sun burning the rocket.
I can see the satellite.
All the stars are brightening up the sky tonight.
I can see a robot that the alien has invented.

Callum Chilton (7)
Greenways Primary School, Stoke-On-Trent

Things In Space

Space is a place where you can see sparkling stars,
You can hear the space bat angel dragon
Singing among the stars,
Space is where you see galaxies,
They are like spinning stars,
Rockets go *whoosh!* up into space,
Can you see the stars in the sky from Earth?
Stars are a lovely thing to look at,
Have you ever seen a rocket fly off into space?

When you are in a rocket
You can see the solar system
Like a beaming beast.

Hugo Hart (7)
Greenways Primary School, Stoke-On-Trent

Amazing Space

Space is fun and dark
There are aliens and planets
You can see the air and the ground
And lovely music coming from the space angel dragon
You can see a blooming planet like chocolate
People down below can see stars but not you.

So up in space
Is the moon like cheese.
But not many people go up in space.
Animals from a long time ago went up,
There's lots to do and play with.

You've got to have some fun
On the moon.

In space is 1,000 aliens
And you should know there is no food.

Sienna Hallam (7)
Greenways Primary School, Stoke-On-Trent

What It's Like To Be In Space

Stars spin just like Saturn
The space bat angel dragon is singing calmly
The sun is shining brightly
Rockets *vroom vroom* around the sky
With fire burning underneath
The Milky Way shining, twinkle, twinkle
Jupiter is brown waiting in the sky
Astronauts zooming in the rockets
Mars is red with lava all over it
Saturn is spinning just like The Smiler at Alton Towers
It's dark and dull, also scary
Earth is a planet we live on
Different places that I can't explain
'Al al,' says the alien, my friend.

Remy Rowson (8)
Greenways Primary School, Stoke-On-Trent

The Moon

In my rocket
I can see the moon and a satellite,
It is dark and weird.
I am scared like an ant,
The moon is bigger than me.
I can see spacemen on the moon,
And flying saucers swishing everywhere,
It is mad. I wonder if they are having fun,
But I am still scared of meeting them,
It feels like I am a stranger.
The moon is bright and colossal
It is like a massive circle
And my head is like a sieve.
I can see a galaxy,
It is redder than the sun but not hotter than the sun,
If you think it is yellow, it is not.

Finlay Shore (7)
Greenways Primary School, Stoke-On-Trent

Super Space

Super space everywhere
With absolutely no air
Rockets whooshing up and up
As we have some tea in a cup
Twinkling stars out and about
Hopefully we don't have to shout
Alien spaceships straight from Mars
And planets far beyond the stars
The sun feels very hot
And It will never fit in a tiny pot
Super scientific space
I guess it really is quite ace.

Caitlin Spiller (8)
Greenways Primary School, Stoke-On-Trent

A Journey Into Outer Space

Space is calm and peaceful,
Darkness all around us like a whirlpool.
Stars are shooting past us,
Faster and faster and faster,
Even faster than a cheetah.
Saturn is spinning,
Zip, zip, zip!
Stars are sparkling and shooting,
All around us, *whoosh!*
Mars is having an alien invasion,
'Watch out!'
Meteorites are flying,
At the speed of lightning.
An astronaut has just landed,
And put a big flag in the middle of the moon,
Made out of cheese, yum, yum.

Isabel Carter (7)
Greenways Primary School, Stoke-On-Trent

The Wonderful World Of Space

Space is beautiful
Space is massive and enormous
Rockets launch into space
And explore the moon and Mars
About five times a day
Earth is our home
Earth looks like a tiny pebble
When we're in the sky
Most rockets have satellites attached to them
A lot of planets are different colours
Like Mars is red and Pluto is white
Some people think aliens live on Mars.

Jay Edwards (8)
Greenways Primary School, Stoke-On-Trent

In Space

The space bat angel dragon, singing in the air
Up in space there is no gravity
When you look out at your rocket you can see Pluto
The rocket blasts into the gleaming space.

Space is amazing because there are shooting stars
When you look out of your window you can see Jupiter
You should see Pluto, how small it is
Pluto is one of the smallest planets.

I can see an alien waving at me
Pluto is a dwarf star that you can see
We are astronauts floating in the white rocket
Earth is green and light blue.

I can see the satellite when I look out of the window
You can see all of the rocks in the sky.

Jack William Stafford Challinor (7)
Greenways Primary School, Stoke-On-Trent

Amazing Planets

Up in space with all the planets
Mars, it is the rockiest planet
Redder than liquid that comes out of a cut hand
Redder than blazing lava.

Jupiter bluer than the sky
Bluer than the waving sea
Bluer than bright blue clouds.

Saturn, a stripy planet
Stripier than a stripier jumper.

Pluto, the smallest planet
Of all of the planets.

Earth, the planet we live on,
5, 4, 3, 2, 1, blast-off!

Ryan Howard (8)
Greenways Primary School, Stoke-On-Trent

Out Of This World

Space is blue and black
The dark space is all around us
All the twinkly stars are so bright
They are making my eyes hurt so much
I feel like a rocket is blasting off of Earth
I wonder if I will make alien friends
Do you want to do it too?
I think I'm going to like it here
I might not want to go away
I think I'm going to like it a lot
I see the Milky Way
Look at all the stars.

Tara Paterson (8)
Greenways Primary School, Stoke-On-Trent

Twinkling Stars

Stars twinkle in the starry sky
I whizz past the planets
Oh I see it in my eye
That bright planet
I can smell that fresh planet so far away
Oh how I wish I could hold it
I can see that special shooting star
I can see that big planet, Mars
I can see lots of rockets floating by
Stars look at me, with their bright eyes
Aliens talk to me in a funny way.

Lucy Bennion (7)
Greenways Primary School, Stoke-On-Trent

Space Is Everywhere

Space is a beautiful place to be
Aliens walking everywhere
Down on Earth people think
In space you don't have to think
About anything because space is so peaceful
Space is everywhere
Rockets fly, flashing, flaming so fast
The sun burns like a sizzling fish
When you're in a rocket
What can you see?
I can see a star, Mars and the moon.

Zak Rushton (8)
Greenways Primary School, Stoke-On-Trent

In Space I Can See . . .

I am floating in space,
And I can see all the planets and stars flying in the sky,
I can see Mars as red as a rose.
I can see the sun as big as a bun
But hotter and hotter.
All the stars are twinkling in the pitch-black sky,
The moon is white as snow glowing in the moonlight.
I can see the stars shining like the sun.

I am on Mars and I am playing aliens,
Well I'm eating chocolate bars.

Celina Monique Schwartz (8)
Greenways Primary School, Stoke-On-Trent

Shooting Stars

Stars are shining in the night,
The Earth shines in the bright.

Sun is very hot like fire,
The Earth's blue looks like electric wire.

The moon is white,
The rocket is tight.

I can see a satellite,
I can hear my rocket,
I have spare stuff in my pocket.

Paris Marie Mountford (8)
Greenways Primary School, Stoke-On-Trent

All About Space

Space is amazing and astronauts make friends.
You even float like a bird.

There is no gravity in space.
Milky Way and Earth are the best places.

But in space the rockets go at some pace.
They go straight up and up.
You can hear *whoosh!* as you go into the amazing place.

The space bat angel dragon is floating up there.
Aliens are wondering where everybody is.

Liam Brazier (8)
Greenways Primary School, Stoke-On-Trent

Me And My Rocket

We see the Earth,
It looks like it is in our hands,
We are far, far away from it,
So it is very, very small.
We see the shooting stars whooshing past,
We see the space bat angel just sitting there,
On the moon, singing away, a lovely tune.
When we leave I can see all of the smoke.
Someone is coughing
I see a spaceman floating by.

Portia Emily Stanfield (8)
Greenways Primary School, Stoke-On-Trent

Super Stars

Space is a dark place,
People floating in the air.
Blue patterns like the ocean blue.
Yellow stars, like little pieces of the sun floating all over space.
People in rockets looking at all the beautiful stars.
Rockets floating around.
People flying past planets.
Satellites flying in space.
People flying round in space.
Stars shooting past you.

Harrison Kirkham (8)
Greenways Primary School, Stoke-On-Trent

Space Is Cool

The space bat angel dragon finds you
When you are asleep
There are thousands of stars
That light your way
As you glide in space
Rockets blast off into the scary sky
Will millions of stars
Light the sky?
Space is cool,
Space is dark with a bit of light.

Penny Mountford (7)
Greenways Primary School, Stoke-On-Trent

Bright Star

The Earth is spinning around,
The sun is shining like a star,
Some rockets are on the moon,
The moon is cold like ice.

The stars are flashing all the time,
The Milky Way is turning.

The shooting stars are coming past my window,
Astronauts are on the moon,
Loads of stars in space.

Lexie Lakin (7)
Greenways Primary School, Stoke-On-Trent

Free In Space

In space you can see black holes
As the rocket goes the fire fizzes out of the engine
Whoosh! in space.
I can see Pluto
And a rocket and astronauts waving at me, me, me.
Space is black and twinkly
A space that never ends, ends, ends,
The moon is white with little white holes.

Sebastian Franch Pearce (7)
Greenways Primary School, Stoke-On-Trent

About Space

Rockets are flying up
Earth is round and magic
Astronauts are collecting moondust
The moon is like a big ball of cheese
Mars is like burning fire
Saturn has a Milky Way around it
The sun is burning hot.

Faith Jones (7)
Greenways Primary School, Stoke-On-Trent

The Wonderful Space

Space rockets go *whoosh!* up in the air,
There are space bat angel dragons
Flying and singing as they go!
Milky Way, Milky Way,
Everybody wants to eat a Milky Way,
The sun is hot, even hotter, like lava!

Adrian Betts-Nicholson (7)
Greenways Primary School, Stoke-On-Trent

Space

Space is a weird place
The astronauts go in a big rocket
When it goes, it goes *whoosh, whoosh!*
When you are on Saturn
It is a wonderful planet.

Brooklyn Mountford (8)
Greenways Primary School, Stoke-On-Trent

Uh Oh . . .

I bought a lolly yesterday,
Sadly, it was sour,
I took it back into the shop,
But I really had no power.

'There are no other lollies left,'
Is what they said to me,
'There are the lollies over there,
As sour as can be.'

'I do not want a sour lolly!'
That's what I said to them,
They did not really understand,
So I said it all again.

'Have you got some other sweets?'
Is what I also said,
'I also hate the popping candy.
It really hurts my head!'

I only had some pennies left,
So this is what I did,
I ran straight back to my own house,
Went in my room and hid!

Abigail Kulbir Ellen Johns (10)
Hillmorton Primary School, Rugby

The Beautiful Rainforest

The rainforest is very calm,
The chirping of the rare birds,
The feel of the luxurious palm,
The howling of the howler monkeys,

The rampaging rhinos,
The prancing lemurs,
The majestic flamingos,
The drowsy koalas,

The ravenous cheetah,
The plodding giraffe,
The hysteric hyena,
The curious crocodile,

The wondrous water buffalo,
The screeching parrots,
The joyful hippos,
The chattering kookaburras.

Meghan Baker (10)
Hillmorton Primary School, Rugby

Untitled

Lovely cherry lips
Sweet romantic trips

Your eyes glow
When I'm not with you my heart hangs low

Fairies fly high in the skies
Me and you, we tell no lies

I would slay a grizzly bear
So I could stroke your golden hair

You would be sitting in the willow
While I knitted you a pillow

So it would feel like you were in Amarillo.

Caolan Monsell (10)
Hillmorton Primary School, Rugby

Minecraft

Minecraft is a game,
An entertaining one too.
A game with blocks,
To building anything you'd like.
Finding ores,
Building huts,
Having to farm animals,
Build a pack of wolves,
And cats.
Survive Creepers and Zombies,
Kill Endermen,
Build a portal to the Nether,
Kills blazes,
Use a crafting table,
Go to the end,
Kill the Ender Dragon!

Emma Collins (9)
Hillmorton Primary School, Rugby

Friendship

Only friendship is the key,
Always be kind to one another,
Be a good friend to others,
A good friend includes others in games,
You listen carefully to what they have to say,
A loving person makes friendship,
If you want to be treated in a good way
Treat them the way you want to be treated,
You share and care with friends,
Ask questions about their life
And take an interest in others,
Give compliments about others
And don't say unkind things about them,
Friendship bracelets do the job.

Maddie White (8)
Hillmorton Primary School, Rugby

Love Makes A Good Friend

L ove makes your life special in a positive way,
O ur hearts are in our body so we can use them for love,
V aluable friends are what everyone should have,
E xpect the qualities of a heart making friend,

A mazing is the important love which spreads out of your body into
somebody else,

F ear is in your life therefore make sure you have an
understanding friend,
R emember to love someone your heart is clinging to,
I magine that you have no friends,
E njoy the love and peace that you get when people love others,
N ever give up, push yourself and you will finally succeed,
D eep in your soul is the power that will guide you!

Annabelle Kay Setchell (9)
Hillmorton Primary School, Rugby

Cats

Luscious flowing fur
They think they roar
But it is only a purr

A little lion in my house
Slinking around
Hunting bird, shadow and mouse

All sizes
All colours
None the same
Just like humans
Be unique and proud.

Madeleine Ashby (10)
Hillmorton Primary School, Rugby

Alien

Big planets swirling around the sun.
What's that?
Is it an alien saucer?
The aliens go round the planets.
Spotting the sapphire blue ocean
And emerald green land.
When it turns to moonlight,
The two aliens go through Saturn's rings.
Past Jupiter back, back.
Goodbye aliens.
Goodbye.

Holly Ann Lightfoot (8)
Hillmorton Primary School, Rugby

Ivan

I am Ivan
Who was a brave little soul
When I went on a journey that almost didn't end
I faced Starjik's cruel wolves but was never defeated.

I am Ivan
With my teardrops of ice
I got everything I needed
For I am the one who softened Starjik's wintry heart.

I am Ivan
Who brought thy beloved children home.

Carina Vale (8)
Hillmorton Primary School, Rugby

The Day I Saw Snow

The day I saw snow
One by one little snowflakes fluttered down,
Falling on my head to form a crown.

The day I saw snow
It made the dirty grey ground transform
Into a soft white landscape,
And my good friends were throwing snowballs at my cape.

The day I saw snow,
The day drew in, it was time to go,
But luckily for me, Mum was making hot cocoa!

Melyce Easy (11)
Hillmorton Primary School, Rugby

All About Poppet, The Moshi Monster!

She has lovely pink hair
But her skin is always bare.
Poppet is the kindest Moshi of all
And she goes to her favourite stall.
Her best friend is called Katsuma
But she will never like any satsuma.
Sooki-Yaki teaches ninja skills
But Poppet doesn't need to take any pills.

Talia Marples (7)
Hillmorton Primary School, Rugby

My Desert Themed Poem!

The desert is as dry as a bone,
A deadly scorpion shoots across the sand all alone,
The sand is golden and is as hot as ten volcanoes,
The Marathon des Sables would give you blistered toes,
A rare gust of wind blows the barren views,
Sand covering anything and everything too,
It's a lonely environment and rarely sees a peep,
It seems like anything that lives there is always fast asleep.

Ellie Cotton (9)
Hillmorton Primary School, Rugby

Stars

Stars are shining above us,
But we don't see their precious shining light.
Stars are trying to show us
How they are beautiful and bright.
But we don't look up and don't see them
So they just shine for us
Although we don't see their gentle light.

Olga Orlova (9)
Hillmorton Primary School, Rugby

Starjik

Starjik is an evil wizard
Starjik is stuck in a blizzard
Starjik's castle is made of ice
Starjik isn't very nice
Starjik turns people to ice
Starjik loves to have a pie.

Rebekah Finch (8)
Hillmorton Primary School, Rugby

School!

There once was a school
It was so cool
The best day was April Fool's
It's not just cool but super cool
I love school, it's the best.

Kenzie Wilkinson (8)
Hillmorton Primary School, Rugby

Giant Moon

Happy moon
Giant moon
You are a silver one!

Giant moon
Happy moon
What a special one!

Giant moon
Giant moon
Rising in the cold night!

Giant moon
Light moon
What a lovely sight!

Giant moon
Lonely moon
I'll be your friend tonight

And any other night!

You're a special one!
Moon!

Codie Rose (8)
John Shelton Primary School, Coventry

Outer World

Space, o' space
It's ever so big,
It's endless,
Empty, lifeless
And black,
It looks like a void,
Mysterious and unknown,
More than we could ever know.

In space there are comets
With big, long tails
And they can be as huge as a killer whale.
They sparkle as bright as a light in the night,
They're unstoppable, speedy and fast
And go zooming past.

In space there are stars,
A big ball of gas,
They twinkle and are bright,
They are glow, glow, glowing in the night.

In space is a moon but that's quite close,
It has low gravity,
It's rocky and empty.
It's misty and bumpy
And has a silver glow.

In space there are comets,
In space there are stars,
Also a moon
But they're all very far.

Nathan Jones (10)
John Shelton Primary School, Coventry

My Sun

My sun awakens early in the morning,
It shines so bright.
When it is light
My sun makes me feel so happy.

My sun keeps me happy when it's around.
When everyone was in bed
The sun said,
'I'm excited for a new day!'

My sun always hears something quite upsetting,
'Everybody's seen
And nobody's been
To the sun as it seems.'
Which makes the sun say so much!

My sun makes everyone happy
When it is bright
But when the day is over
Everyone goes away.

Aleesha Dionne Cleverley (9)
John Shelton Primary School, Coventry

Untitled

The rocket ship race,
Mars, Jupiter and outer space.
Whizzing through the bejewelled sky
The rocket ships shatter stars into a million pieces.
One spaceship takes the lead,
Not for long.
The bright disco lights shine
And the dance floor shimmers beneath them.
Guests cheer,
All of a sudden . . . *crunch!*
The monstrous beat, the comet destroys the party.
Who won?

Carys Moss (11)
John Shelton Primary School, Coventry

Stars!

Shimmering, shooting stars,
Cracked pieces of glass,
Softly twinkling in the night.

Making pictures, blowing minds,
Stars always make us surprised.
They stay with us through day and night,
Just look and they're there.

Guiding us on journeys,
Away and back home.
Don't be sad because you'll never be alone.

In the sky,
High up crystallised gems
Performing a midnight show for little children's eyes.
When it comes to morning we can't see them,
But we know still that
They are there to stand by us,
Whenever we're alone.

Millie Henderson (10)
John Shelton Primary School, Coventry

Sparkling Stars

She sparkles like a smiling mother,
She runs like she is in a race,
She buzzes like a busy bee.

She is running in space
Or should I say hopping in a race.
She is faster than a cheetah,
Maybe her name is Zita.

She shimmers like light,
She is as bright.
Her name is Zita,
I think she is a cheetah!

Helena Madavana Saiju (9)
John Shelton Primary School, Coventry

Outside The Earth

Outside the Earth is wonderful.
It is an outstanding place.
With all the planets, moon and stars,
That place is called space.

If you went to space,
You would see, among the stars,
The planets Saturn, Jupiter,
Neptune, Venus and Mars.

The stars giggle and giggle.
They love to have fun.
The moon spies on the galaxy around her,
So does the friendly sun.

Astronauts visit to admire the sight,
Of space and the Milky Way.
The planets, sun and moon twirl,
Turn and smile all day, every day!

Amelia Coleman (9)
John Shelton Primary School, Coventry

Shooting Star

Shooting star,
Falling star
Lighting up the sky.

Shooting star,
Falling star
What a sight to see.

Shooting star,
Falling star
Lighting up the night.

Shooting star,
Falling star
Grant a wish for me tonight.

Lilly Johnson (8)
John Shelton Primary School, Coventry

The Sun

It shines like a diamond,
It burns with fire,
It is a wildfire.

It brightens the Earth
And puts a smile
On people's faces who like it.

It feels wild and free
And it is the sound of freedom.

It brings happy faces to villains
And bright good deeds.

It is a home of yellow flowers
Growing day by day
And year by year.

It laughs at the moon clouds
As the sun turns over.

Reagan Johnson (10)
John Shelton Primary School, Coventry

Moon

Moon, moon are you out there?
When I always see you, you seem so fair.
Are you meeting your friend, Sun?
Moon, moon where are you?
You really seem like a big balloon!
I wish I could always walk on you!
You have no water, wind or air
But there is nothing really up there.
When the sun sets you rise up in the blue sky.
Your gravity is weak,
I hear you really have no atmosphere.
But don't be sad moon, please don't cry
For I still love you in the sky.

Emanuela Brown (8)
John Shelton Primary School, Coventry

Space

Shiny, shimmering stars,
Colourful, colossal planets,
Sparkly, speedy comets,
All drifting through the bejewelled sky.

Space is a school full of many unique things,
The shining stars are children playing cheerfully.
The rockets dashing through the dark, never-ending world
Are pencils busy writing.

The mysterious space is a sea full of wonderful creatures.
The black, blank space is the water flowing calmly,
The planets are boats surfing slowly on the precious sea.

Gabriela Gnas (11)
John Shelton Primary School, Coventry

The Milky Way!

White Milky Way
Creamy Milky Way
How did you get so bright?

You are the star this night
For you are a beautiful sight!

White Milky Way
Creamy Milky Way
How do you spin so fast?

Don't be sad I'm here just for you
I'm your friend in the pale blue night.

Naeva Joby (8)
John Shelton Primary School, Coventry

Untitled

Space is a never-ending void
Dotted with little balls of gas.
Zoom! as the comet speeds by
Like a race car.

The moon is a big ball of wool,
Rising when a day ends
And a night begins.

The planets are ancient relics
Never to be moved or stolen.

Samuel Hunter (11)
John Shelton Primary School, Coventry

The Star Poem

S tars shine
T winkling bright
A point at every end
R acing around every night
S tars will never end.

Lewis Smallman (9)
John Shelton Primary School, Coventry

Stars

S tars, stars that glimmer and glow like crystals that shine
T winkling enthusiastically increasing the light
A tranquil, calm setting all the time
R acing and dashing, playing around just like us every night
S lowly shooting they make a glorious sea of comets.

Lavanya Ganeshalingam (8)
John Shelton Primary School, Coventry

Stars

S tars, stars are glimmering crystals
T winkling bright
A tmosphere in the night
R acing high
S parkly, shiny all the time.

Madison Michelle Ayriss (8)
John Shelton Primary School, Coventry

Stars

S tars are sparkling crystals
T winkling brighter and brighter every night
A glimmering shine every evening
R acing through the sky like a racing car
S hiny like they do.

Amy Jane Northall (9)
John Shelton Primary School, Coventry

The Alien

The alien I met was green
And he's a thing you've never seen.
He likes the shiny bling
And he's an alien that is green.

The alien I met was tall
But worst of all
He was scary and hairy
And he had pointy teeth.

His hair was a mess
And he wasn't the best of all the rest.

His breath smelt like rotten eggs,
So stay away from his disgusting breath.

Emily Prodger (10)
Johnstown Junior School, Wrexham

The Aliens In Space

Do you ever wonder
Where aliens come and go?
If you don't I'll tell you so.

This planet called Mars
Is very far away
And this alien called Sara
Will scare you away.

She's as green as gooey slime
Her eyes as red as Devil horns
Her arms as long as rulers
Her mouth as cold as Neptune.

I've been on Mars before
She's never terrified me
Now be careful
She will be there.

Do you ever wonder
Where aliens come and go?
If you don't I'll tell you so.

On this planet called Mercury
It is very nearby and this
Alien called Zoo Zoo will suddenly float by.

He's as white as a polar bear's fur
His eyes as green as long grass
His arms as short as pens
His mouth as blue as the bright sky.

Halle Mitchell (10)
Johnstown Junior School, Wrexham

A-Z Of Outer Space

A lot of people you've never met
B igger than big can get
C omets dashing through the sky
D are to go? You might die!
E xciting new world to explore!
F ollow me through the door . . .

G et in a rocket to the sky
H igher and higher, high, high, high
I land after two days
J umping around in outer space
K eeping samples of rock
L ocking the rocket with a lock
M aking our way back
N ow I'm driving the rocket and getting the knack . . .
O h no! I hear a clack!
P hew! Just small meteors hitting our roof

Q ueens and kings aren't offered this opportunity
R eally something to brag about to your community
S ome fun's been had in outer space
T hink it's been ace
U nder the sun's not fun
V ery much fun's had over the sun!
W hat did he go there to learn today?
eX tra fun can be had when no one's in your way!
Y ou have had fun haven't you? Well, so have I!
Z ooming in a rocket through the sky!

Daisy Hannaby (10)
Johnstown Junior School, Wrexham

Trip To Space

Got out the spaceship
Stepped on a rock
Saw a gloomy block
Or was it a green-headed alien
With 1,000 aliens beside him?
Staring while deciding whether to step forward or not
Went back to the spaceship – it was not there
Turned around and aliens were just there.
Aliens looked at me and said,
'Why are you crying?
Why do you stare, stare, stare?'

As Planet Jupiter was spinning, spinning, spinning
Round for eternity
The aliens were still there
Brought me to their spaceship
Their planet was spinning too, too, too fast
Master Mongo Mongan March shouted as loud as a lion,
'Why are you here?'

I ran away
I got home and always wondered
Why were they there.
Why did they have brown hair?

Nicole Ventura (9)
Johnstown Junior School, Wrexham

Space

S pace is as dark as a black blanket.
P ack your bags we are going to space!
A re you ready to land?
C an we fly to Mercury?
E verybody get ready for countdown!

Jack Minson (9)
Johnstown Junior School, Wrexham

Speech Of The Solar System

Mercury: 'I'm Mercury, the smallest planet, as small as Earth's moon
And I don't spin all the way around very soon.'
Venus: 'Hi, I'm Venus, I've got mountains and volcanoes that spray,
I'm the same size as Earth but spin the opposite way.'
Earth: 'I'm Earth, the home for every boy and girl
But I might also have some tornadoes that swirl!'
Mars: 'I'm Mars,
Like all the other planets I am surrounded by stars.'
Jupiter: 'I'm humongous, gigantic and made of gas and helium
So don't dare to step on me
Or you'll just get sunk right down in my tummy for my tea!'
Saturn: 'Yeah, I'm Saturn, I've got seven rings,
Made of dust, rocks and lots of other things.
If you could fit me in an enormous bath tub then I would float
Just like a boat.'
Uranus: 'An Earth-sized object hit me hard, then I cried
And realised that I was lying on my side.'
Neptune: 'I've got millions of storms and I'm also mysterious
So bring an umbrella, I'm serious.'

Helin Topal (11)
Johnstown Junior School, Wrexham

When The Alien Stole My Socks

The alien was running to my gloomy room,
He stole my gloomy socks
And ran away with my socks
And went to the planet Venus to live,
I never saw my socks again,
I was so excited because . . .

They were made of water
And they were dirty,
With a chicken
Inside the stinky
Giant socks.

Ewan Roberts (10)
Johnstown Junior School, Wrexham

My Alien!

My alien is not scary, glooming and glowing.
All he dreams is to see the stars of the Milky Way shimmer and shine.
His name is Kyle, he lives far, far away where the stars do not shine.
I always wonder where he wanders far and wide.
His eyes like a twinkling star.
My alien may be shy, very kind
And he can sort you out before thunder can strike.
He has a very strange appetite, no wonder he is strange.

His teeth are not clean
I wonder if he owns a toothbrush!
He has two beaming eyes
And four long legs.
He is purple and blue,
He has two small, small ears.

He promised me one day he
Would take me to his birthplace.
So I swore that one day
We would go and see the stars of the Milky Way.

Kasey Paige Roberts (10)
Johnstown Junior School, Wrexham

Out Of This World

Out of this world is space,
Such a wonderful, wonderful place,
It is like a ginormous maze
Which makes you gaze for days,
It is so fun,
Because all the planets orbit the sun,
Mercury, Venus, Earth and Mars
Can all see the stars,
Jupiter, Saturn, Uranus and Neptune
All at least have one moon,
Space, such a magical place.

Emily-May Hughes (10)
Johnstown Junior School, Wrexham

All About Aliens

Have you ever wondered
If somewhere in this world
There's a planet made of thunder
It makes me want to burn.

I've never really thought
That they could have fought
The aliens from Mount Zion
That look a bit like a lion.

On the planet Zennox
Live the Twooky brothers
A pair of aliens
They are as hairy as a bear.

The final planet is the Cabbothey
With a pair of aliens called the Wooshys
But all these aliens want one friend
So if you're passing make them proud
Be their friends and you'll be sound.

Amy Anne Jones (10)
Johnstown Junior School, Wrexham

The Demon Destroyer's Invasion

There is an invasion coming,
It is larger than the sun,
Larger than any planet in the solar system,
Galactus is here with a huge hungry tum.

Danger, danger!
Invasion, invasion!
Galactus, Galactus here!

Galactus, Galactus
Here, here
Demolish, demolish
The planet, the planet!

Thomas Hodgkiss (10)
Johnstown Junior School, Wrexham

73

A Trip To Space

O ut of this world is space
U p above the stars is a magical place
T ell everyone you know

O ut of this world glows
F ollow the never-ending path

T alk as you joke and laugh
H ave all the fun you want
I n this magical portal in space
S pace is full of fun

W hat an interesting place to be
O ver and over it never stops
R emember not to get lost
L ots of lovely planets orbit around the Earth
D on't let the pretty colours fool you!

Lowri Jean Pottage (11)
Johnstown Junior School, Wrexham

The Mysterious Aliens

In the solar system,
In the gloomy and starless solar system,
On the magnificent planet called Alien Planet Mars
All the aliens are gloomy
And some aliens are slimy.
If you put roasting fire on them
They would melt
But there is an alien,
A slimy and stinky king alien called Rubix.
Now Rubix is a marvellous king
And always a king,
But there is something wrong.
Oh no! Not the mysterious aliens,
Sound the alarm,
Beep! Beep! Beep! Beep!

Ryan Edge (9)
Johnstown Junior School, Wrexham

The Sky Is Our Dream

The northern sky down below shines brighter than the sun,
Stars gleaming through the sky,
Bulging planets with storms on high,
Great comets speeding around us,
Every time scattering asteroids all around us.
Time to land, I put on my suit,
But what's happened? The engine will not start,
An asteroid comes towards us,
We're going to die,
I yell from the top of my voice, 'Asteroid, asteroid!'
I get the engine working
We're coming back home,
My heart was racing but now I'm fine.

Ben Wynn
Johnstown Junior School, Wrexham

The Terrible Alien

One terrible time a tiny terrible alien lived on Alien Paradise
It is dusty and dark
So if you go it will give you a fright.

The terrible alien of course I have seen him before
He will scare you and tear you
So never go near him.
If you go to him you may not go home.
If you do go home
It must be luck.

His name is Terrible Ted,
He is terrible as you can tell by his name.
Remember I told you so.

Ryan Price (10)
Johnstown Junior School, Wrexham

75

My Alien Friends

My alien friends are really funny,
My alien friends feel odd in the tummy,
They dance about and prance around just like a kangaroo,
They love to watch the Milky Way go by every single day.

They love to sing each other's names
Like Slippery Sid, Angry Alice and Crazy Cameron.
My alien friends are too silly.
My alien friends love to see the sun look like a golden penny.

My alien friends aren't bullies.
My alien friends are all buddies.
Even though they're not like me
They're still all my alien buddies.

Rachael Hatton (9)
Johnstown Junior School, Wrexham

Space

O uter space is a mysterious place
U p in the world
T he sun is the centre of the solar system
E xotic planets
R iding around in the rocket

S pace is a wondrous place
P lanets are millions of miles away from the sun
A mazing world
C an you believe this world?
E very day is a new day in space.

Libby Condren (10)
Johnstown Junior School, Wrexham

What Am I?

Life-bringer
Boat-eater
Land-crusher
Temperature-masher
Time-evolver
Sun-orbiter
Planet-topper.

I am Earth.

Billy Wynne (11)
Johnstown Junior School, Wrexham

Space

S aturn is the biggest and brightest planet
P luto is now a dwarf planet
A liens . . . well we will forget about them
C reating new rockets to launch into space
E arth is the planet we live on!

Jack Edwards (9)
Johnstown Junior School, Wrexham

Planet Earth

E very day new life is made
A stronauts get ready to come home
R ocks and comets flying through space
T itan . . . the main moon of Saturn
H umongous stars slowly orbit the planets.

Jack Williams (11)
Johnstown Junior School, Wrexham

Super Starry Space

S himmering, shiny space
P lanets rotating around the sun
A mazing space shining and shimmering
C rashing comets crashing down to Earth
E xciting new worlds to explore.

Emily Kynaston (10)
Johnstown Junior School, Wrexham

Space Acrostic – Haiku

S pace is marvellous
U nderneath the unknown space
N ow we live on Earth.

Kyle Elwyn Williams (10)
Johnstown Junior School, Wrexham

Space

What am I?
I like space
I am gooey
I hate sun
I laugh a lot
I hate humans
I like jumping
I bounce a lot
I can't speak.

An alien.

Jayden Dwight (8)
Jubilee Academy Mossley, Walsall

Adventure Time!

A n amazing time in space
D arkness with shiny stars
V enus is a planet
E arth is spinning
N ight is when aliens come out
T wo astronauts are bouncing on the moon
U nder the moon are creepy aliens
R ocks are everywhere
E xtremely tired, time to head off home.

Demileigh Nicklin (7)
Jubilee Academy Mossley, Walsall

Man On The Moon

A liens have googly eyes
L anding on the moon is an astronaut
I n space a man is floating
E yes are green, also are spooky
N ow the aliens are destroyed, now the world is saved
S o the planet is saved, one day they will strike again.

Ryan Tupper (7)
Jubilee Academy Mossley, Walsall

The Life In Space

S tars are shooting all over the place
P lanet Earth is one of the biggest planets in space
A stronauts are checking out the amazing space
C annon balls that are in the air explode in space . . .
E xcited astronauts cannot wait to go to the moon.

Stevie-Jo Andrews (7)
Jubilee Academy Mossley, Walsall

Stars

S ilent rocket
T alented alien
A liens are slimy
R ippled rocket
S tars are twinkly.

Brandon Lei Wainwright (8)
Jubilee Academy Mossley, Walsall

Alien, Alien

A liens are slimy
L ights are shining from the purple clouds
I ncredible aliens are clever
E arth spins round and round
N ow the aliens are creepy when they have sharp teeth.

Georgie Alan James Sagent (8)
Jubilee Academy Mossley, Walsall

Earth Is Spinning

E arth is spinning round and round up to the sun, down to
the ground
A liens are creepy in the darkness, dazzling sun
R ace to attack
T hunder has begun
H ere I am on the crashing, fake moon.

Tahlina Marcia Francis Hall (8)
Jubilee Academy Mossley, Walsall

Alien

A ll cheese
L ots of eyes
I s this where you live?
E arth, nice to meet you
N ight-time is black.

John Memela (7)
Jubilee Academy Mossley, Walsall

Castle Dragons Kennings

Fire breather
Castle killer
Scaly scarer
Flame-thrower.

Night killer
Sheep eater
Flapping flyer
Scary destroyer.

Knight frightener
Castle slayer
Mean fire-breather
Greedy gobbler.

Beastly eater
Wood breaker
People hurter
Castle attacker.

Aimee Paine (8)
Manor Hill First School, Stone

Daring Dragons

Scaly scarer
Fire-breather
Knight killer.

Sheep eater
High flyer
Greedy gobbler
Castle attacker.

Beastly battler
Fire maker
Castle breaker
Forest burner.

Castle grumbler
Flame-thrower
Mean muncher.

Bradley Appleton (9)
Manor Hill First School, Stone

The Royal Castle

C astles I see deep in the woods
A fter going through the woods you'll see the biggest castle in the world
S tay for a day, you'll like it
T onight is the royal ball, stay for a cup or two
L ovely day to see the king and queen
E at and eat, that's what the king does. Hope you like the castle, I like it too.

Lily-May Starr (9)
Manor Hill First School, Stone

Attack!

C reeping guards all through the night
A xe-throwing attackers charging at the castle
S inking attackers in the freezing deep moat
'T ear apart that castle!' is what all the attackers say
L ands are silent with fear
E nough of the attacking, more defending.

Bobby Baines (9)
Manor Hill First School, Stone

Galaxy

G iant planets like Jupiter have lots of water and not much land
A liens are not real and seem very scary
L unar rock is something hard to find on the moon
A stronauts travel into space and spend many years training to
go there
X -rays could be needed to check if
Y ou get hurt.

Ayanna Gayle (7)
Perry Beeches Infant School, Birmingham

Galaxy

G as giant planets have lots of water and not much surface
A liens are not real but they do look scary
L unar rock is very hard to find on the moon
A stronauts spend many years training to go into space
X -rays might be needed if you get hurt in the spaceship
Y ellow objects in space are called stars. The sun is the biggest
star in our solar system.

Harjas Kaur Tung (7)
Perry Beeches Infant School, Birmingham

Neptune

N eptune is a stormy planet
E arth is green and blue
P luto is not a planet and it is the furthest from the sun
T itan is Saturn's moon
U ranus is very cold
N eptune is a gas giant
E arth is green and blue and it is two colours.

Hennessy Dennis-Hayes (7)
Perry Beeches Infant School, Birmingham

Neptune

N eptune is the second coldest planet
E arth is the planet everyone lives on
P luto is a planet but not in our solar system
T itan is Saturn's moon
U ranus is the coldest planet
N eptune is an icy gas giant
E arth is a planet with land and sea.

Jimmy Fox (7)
Perry Beeches Infant School, Birmingham

Jupiter

J upiter, the biggest planet in our solar system, it's a gas giant
U ranus is the icy gas giant
P luto is not a planet
I n our solar system there are eight planets
T he tiny planet is Mercury
E arth is green, white and blue
R ockets have a sharp point at the front.

Dicaprio Levy (7)
Perry Beeches Infant School, Birmingham

Saturn

S hiny stars are in the sky
A stronauts walked on the moon
T he sun and all the stars we see in the night sky belong to a
galaxy called the Milky Way
U ranus is an icy gas giant
R ocket flies in space
N eptune's a cold windy planet.

Riyad Ahmed (7)
Perry Beeches Infant School, Birmingham

Uranus

U ranus is the coldest planet in the solar system and it has got
icy rings around it
R ockets can go into space and they can go far away
A liens can go in space
N eptune is a planet in the solar system
U ranus is a cold planet
S tars are up in the night when we are sleeping.

Harkirt Kapoor (7)
Perry Beeches Infant School, Birmingham

Rockets

R ocky moon far from Earth where Neil stopped
O n the moon are big rocks
C an Neil push them over?
K eep calm, there's no aliens
E very step of the way is dusty
T ransport me back to Earth.

Kira Mitchell (6)
Perry Beeches Infant School, Birmingham

Rocket

R ocks on the moon are so hard
O n the moon aliens travel everywhere
C ome to Mars because it is a nice place
K eep safe in space because it may be dangerous
E arth is full of people and shops
T winkly stars are so shiny.

Havwa Syed (6)
Perry Beeches Infant School, Birmingham

Rocket

R acing rockets flying in dark space
O n the moon it's very quiet
C an we live on the moon?
K eep safe in space
E arth is a big blue-green planet
T here's no oxygen in space.

Adeeb Haidari (6)
Perry Beeches Infant School, Birmingham

Stars

S aturn has icy rings around it to protect it
T iny planet, it used to be Pluto
A liens live in space because no aliens live on the Earth
R ockets go into space because they want to see all the
  beautiful planets
S hiny stars are in the beautiful sky.

Thomas Mobbs (6)
Perry Beeches Infant School, Birmingham

Rockets

R ocket races in the sky
O n the moon there is an alien eating pie
C an't go up, can't go down
K eeps on spinning round and round
E nd it now I want to go home
T o Earth so I'm not alone.

Layla Keay (6)
Perry Beeches Infant School, Birmingham

Saturn

S aturn is very stripy
A nd Saturn is icy and very cold
T itan is Saturn's little moon
U ranus is next to Saturn
R ings of ice and dust
N eptune has rings like Saturn.

Finley Cafferkey (7)
Perry Beeches Infant School, Birmingham

Planets

P lanets whizzing round and round
L ily the astronaut in the big shiny rocket
A stronauts flying everywhere
N ight is dark and gloomy
E arth turning round and round
T aking big moon rocks back to Earth.

Sidney James Corry (7)
Perry Beeches Infant School, Birmingham

Planets

P lanning to go to the moon
L ooking out for aliens
A liens killing people on the moon
N eptune is the furthest planet away from the sun
E vil aliens after people
T he moon shining at night.

Karla Poulton (6)
Perry Beeches Infant School, Birmingham

Saturn

S tars shine at night
A liens live on the moon
T itan is Saturn's biggest moon
U ranus is the coldest planet in our solar system
R ocky red Mars
N eptune has lots of storms.

Jamie Ian Millichap (6)
Perry Beeches Infant School, Birmingham

Space

S hooting stars shining like twinkling diamonds
P luto has now shrunk and is called a dwarf planet
A steroids walking with no gravity, you might land on the
  closest planet
C louds of poisonous ash from Venus, be careful you might land
  on it
E arth is my planet because I live there and so do all of you.

Jannat Simaab Saqib (6)
Perry Beeches Infant School, Birmingham

Saturn

S aturn
A liens can fly in rockets
T itan is its largest moon
U ranus is a planet
R ockets can fly
N eptune is a planet.

Ayush Sangar (6)
Perry Beeches Infant School, Birmingham

Planet

P lanets spin in space
L ittle Pluto is a small planet
A stronauts are people
N eptune is the furthest from the sun
E arth has a moon
T ry to get to the moon.

Tyler Roy Joseph Hollington (6)
Perry Beeches Infant School, Birmingham

Space

U ranus has icy cold rings around it
R ocket can go into space
A liens live on the moon
N eptune is a cold planet
U ranus is the cold planet
S un is hot.

Summer-Lea Watts (6)
Perry Beeches Infant School, Birmingham

Space

S hining star twinkling bright
P lanets in space everywhere
A stronauts floating in space
C alling aliens from the ship
E rupting volcanoes very hot.

Deen Akhtar (6)
Perry Beeches Infant School, Birmingham

Space

S olar system has planets in space
P luto is the smallest planet
A liens are flying in a UFO
C alling aliens in space
E arth is where real people live.

Mahdi Choudhury (7)
Perry Beeches Infant School, Birmingham

Space

S tars are twinkling in the sky
P luto is the smallest planet
A steroids hitting the moon
C omets are nice to look at
E arth is good to live on.

Grace Cafferkey (7)
Perry Beeches Infant School, Birmingham

Space

S tars are twinkling in the sky
P lanets are exciting to look at
A stronauts are floating on the moon
C louds of acid are poisonous
E arth is where you live, this is where I live.

Leah Bent (7)
Perry Beeches Infant School, Birmingham

Space

S hiny stars make different sounds so people enjoy it
P luto is the smallest planet in our solar system
A liens landing on the moon
C omets in space
E arth has life.

Sufiyaan Hussain (6)
Perry Beeches Infant School, Birmingham

Space

S aturn has ice and dust around it
P luto is now known as a dwarf planet
A liens are lurking behind other planets
C raters are ready to get crashed
E arth is where all of us live.

Oliver Jones (7)
Perry Beeches Infant School, Birmingham

Space

S pace is very dangerous
P luto is a dwarf planet
A liens floating all around space
C omets floating around space
E arth is where I live and so do all of you.

Tia Thompson (6)
Perry Beeches Infant School, Birmingham

Star

S tars twinkle at night-time
T itan is Saturn's biggest moon
A stronauts have been on the moon, aliens talk on the moon
  and talk babyish
R ockets can fly to the moon, astronauts can jump on the moon.

Maddison Nolan (6)
Perry Beeches Infant School, Birmingham

Space

S olar system full of planets
P luto is known as a dwarf planet
A stronauts heading everywhere
C omets flying through the sky
E arth is very, very fantastic!

Zain Khan (7)
Perry Beeches Infant School, Birmingham

Space

S olar system is made up of planets in space
P lanets are all around the Earth
A stronauts think Jupiter has 16 moons
C omets fly in space all day and night
E rupting volcano on Venus.

Mackenzie Parry (7)
Perry Beeches Infant School, Birmingham

Space

S hooting stars flying by
P luto is the smallest planet
A stronauts floating by
C alling aliens
E rupting volcanoes.

Muneeb Rehman (7)
Perry Beeches Infant School, Birmingham

Space

S pace is full of planets
P luto is the smallest planet
A stronauts send micro buggies into space
C omets float around space
E arth is where I live and so do you.

Lyla-Rose Wilson (6)
Perry Beeches Infant School, Birmingham

Space

S hining in the sky
P luto is a small planet
A liens are floating up
C omets are spinning around
E arth is a good planet in space.

Hamza Qadeer (7)
Perry Beeches Infant School, Birmingham

Space

S tars are twinkling, every one
P lanets are large in space
A ll of the other planets have a bit of moon
C an you go into space?
E arth has water and people.

Ismail Ali (7)
Perry Beeches Infant School, Birmingham

Space

S hiny stars are everywhere
P luto is the furthest planet from the sun
A stronauts are in space
C areful, you might hit a planet
E arth is having a battle with another planet.

Finley Williams (7)
Perry Beeches Infant School, Birmingham

Aliens

A stronauts from Earth far and wide
L ittle cheeky alien where are you?
I 've hunted and hunted for you everywhere
E zie Ezie that's your name, green as glue
N inety-nine years I've been searching for you.

Adam Moustakim
Perry Beeches Infant School, Birmingham

Mars

M ars is a hotter planet than Earth
A liens live on planets in stories and astronauts go into space
R ockets fly into space, the first rocket made belonged to
    Buzz Aldrin
S trong Mars has three volcanoes and it is made from ice. It is
    really, really strong and the planet belongs to the solar system.

Lola Frances Bebbington-Grice (7)
Perry Beeches Infant School, Birmingham

Space

S uper brave spacemen in a rocket.
P luto, the last and coldest planet.
A liens . . . are there such things?
C *rash!* An asteroid just hit the moon!
E arth is my favourite planet because you and me both live here.

Bruce Stevenson (7)
Perry Beeches Infant School, Birmingham

Space

S lithery alien came on the moon, I was scared, my legs
  were shaking
P lanets are real but not Pluto, it is too small to collect other objects
A stronauts train to go to the moon
C racking moon
E arth is where we live.

Insaf Moustakim (6)
Perry Beeches Infant School, Birmingham

Space

S olar system has all eight planets
P luto is the smallest planet in the solar system
A liens are slimy and they live on Mars
C omet aiming to come at Earth
E nergy to go to the planets.

Tionne Critchlow-Woyo (7)
Perry Beeches Infant School, Birmingham

Space

S hooting rocket going up to space
P erhaps landing up on the moon
A stronauts panicking around in case there are any aliens
C ongratulations, we made it to the moon
E nd it now, I want to go home to Earth.

Evie Jones (6)
Perry Beeches Infant School, Birmingham

Space

S hooting stars sparkling in the sky
P lanets all around me colourful and bright
A stronauts in the dark night sky
C an I land on the white rocky moon?
E vil aliens passing by.

Lilly-Mae Morris (7)
Perry Beeches Infant School, Birmingham

Space

S olar system is the biggest place in the world
P luto is the smallest planet in space
A liens are floating in space and aliens see shooting stars
C omets in space
E arth is a very good planet.

Mahir Majid (6)
Perry Beeches Infant School, Birmingham

Space

S hining, shimmering stars like a diamond in the sky
P luto is the smallest planet in our solar system
A stronauts walking out in space
C ome out in space with me
E arth is my planet and yours too.

Amelia South (7)
Perry Beeches Infant School, Birmingham

Alien

A stronauts fly in space in a rocket
L unar is a type of moon like Titan
I n space there are eight planets in our solar system
E verybody can go in space
N eptune is purple and light blue.

Jessica Slack (7)
Perry Beeches Infant School, Birmingham

Space

S hooting stars in the sky
P lanets are all around the sun
A stronauts go in a rocket into space
C ome to space everybody
E arth is light blue.

Grace Beresford (7)
Perry Beeches Infant School, Birmingham

Space

S pace is so amazing and beautiful
P eople can't go to the sun
A stronauts fly into space
C omets are floating around space
E arth is where everyone lives.

Taylor Jane Bingham (6)
Perry Beeches Infant School, Birmingham

Space

S hining stars by the moon
P lanets spinning near you
A stronauts walking slowly on the moon
C an you come home please? I beg you
E ating cheese before they go 3, 2, 1, blast-off, I loved it so.

Millie Claire Boulton (7)
Perry Beeches Infant School, Birmingham

Space

S parkly moon twinkling in the sky
P retty stars shining in space
A stronauts go around all the planets
C omets are small and fast
E arth is my planet.

Lily-Ella Adams (7)
Perry Beeches Infant School, Birmingham

Aliens

A stronauts big and strong, on a rocket off they go
L and on the moon, there is no one around
I n the deep holes astronauts hold their breath
E nergetic aliens, 1,000 eyes, disgusting green slime
N asty aliens seek out astronauts. Oh no!

Shiyaad Ali (6)
Perry Beeches Infant School, Birmingham

Space

S uper space, dangerous sun and Venus
P luto is the smallest planet
A liens are scary on the moon
C omets aiming to crash into something
E arth is the luckiest planet.

Harjot Singh (7)
Perry Beeches Infant School, Birmingham

Space

S hining sun so hot and bright
P ast the Earth to the moon
A liens say hi to be polite
C omets fly and shoot across the sky
E xpanding space and find new planets.

Raiven Mabbett (7)
Perry Beeches Infant School, Birmingham

Space

S tars are twinkling in the sky, you can see them very high
P lanets are different to each other
A liens are in space
C ome to the moon
E arth is the same size as Venus.

Teagan Jelfs-Mione (6)
Perry Beeches Infant School, Birmingham

Stars

S parkly stars shooting into space
T ravelling into dark space, stars making it shine
A star called the wishing star is spinning into space
R ings around Saturn, ice cold and slippery
S omething's shooting into space, making space shine up.

Tosin Salami (6)
Perry Beeches Infant School, Birmingham

Stars

S tars twinkling in the black sky
T aking green aliens one by one
A spooky alien flying in space
R ocket flying to the moon
S tars are really lovely in the sky.

Charlie Foster (6)
Perry Beeches Infant School, Birmingham

Stars

S tars twinkle and stars are shiny
T he stars show the astronauts the way
A liens land by the stars
R ockets whiz to Mars
S tars light up the sky.

Riyad Rahman (6)
Perry Beeches Infant School, Birmingham

Space

S parkly stars in the dark sky
P lanets turn around each other
A stronauts go to the planets
C omets are a piece of rock
E arth is close to Mars.

Lexi Hope Christian (6)
Perry Beeches Infant School, Birmingham

Space

S olar systems with Pluto
P luto is a small planet
A poisonous acid on Mercury
C omet, Earth, rock, asteroids
E arth is a nice planet to live on.

Daniel Joseph (6)
Perry Beeches Infant School, Birmingham

Aliens

A way we go to the crater moon and red Mars
L et's go on a dark space adventure
I t's hard to spot the green aliens
E arth, I wish you came with me
N eptune's colour is cold blue.

Dayna Evans (7)
Perry Beeches Infant School, Birmingham

Aliens

A brilliant moon
L ittle green aliens
I n their UFOs
E xploring spaceman
N eptune is the last planet.

Keanu Reid (7)
Perry Beeches Infant School, Birmingham

Stars

S tarry stars up high
T ravelling to the moon
A very funky alien with three eyes or two
R eally, really dark up high
S tarry, starry stars in the sky.

Amidat Oluwaseun Amidu (7)
Perry Beeches Infant School, Birmingham

Mars

M ars is a rocky red planet
A liens are very green and sometimes they are different colours
R ocky volcanoes are on the red planet, Mars
S hiny stars are twinkling in the sky.

Isla Mai Lawson (7)
Perry Beeches Infant School, Birmingham

Mars

M ars is in the solar system
A stronauts are in space
R ockets are in space but I've never been in one
S pace is really high in the sky.

Dayyan Miah (6)
Perry Beeches Infant School, Birmingham

Mars

M ars is very rocky
A liens are not real on Mars
R ed planet is Mars
S tars shine bright at night.

Jaida Porter (6)
Perry Beeches Infant School, Birmingham

Mars

M ars is a red rocky planet
A liens are from outer space
R ockets go to outer space
S aturn is a giant, icy planet.

Harvey Harte (6)
Perry Beeches Infant School, Birmingham

Star

S hiny stars sparkle at night in the dark sky
T iny planets and stars are in the solar system
A stronauts visit the moon and other planets
R ockets can go into space.

Joel Harris (6)
Perry Beeches Infant School, Birmingham

Outer Space

Stars shooting across the space shuttle,
Making your insides all flimsy and rattle.
On my way, I see Planet Mercury,
Right near the sun
So hot like a hot cross bun.
Then I pass Planet Mars,
Surrounded by all the shiny stars,
Which reminds me of my favourite chocolate bars.

Sebastian Kimblin (7)
Priory School, Birmingham

Stars And Planets

The sun is big, hot and round,
The stars are shining and shooting
Like the speed of sound.
The planets are colourful
And of all different sizes.
The astronaut is flying as his spaceship rises.
Rockets shining like the sun,
Glancing from the horizon one by one.

Joshua Pritchard (10)
Priory School, Birmingham

Magic In Space

A star is bright, shiny and small,
A comet is a fast, speedy lightning ball.
The aliens are short, round but slim,
The planets are all colourful but sometimes dim.
The flying saucer is fast and strange,
The moon is full of craters of a wide range.

Patrick Purcell-Jones (8)
Priory School, Birmingham

Czech Me Out!

It's not much of a secret,
But not everybody knows.
You can't tell from my accent,
You can't tell from my clothes.
I'm a bit like fish and chips,
I'm a slice of bábovka.
Everyone knows I'm a Hill,
Do you know I'm Rakowska?
Czech summers are always hot,
And winters bring deep, deep snow.
To the river in the sun,
And winter sledging we go.
I do like being English,
With my English family,
But don't forget I am Czech,
I am happy being me.

Elena Hill (9)
SS Peter & Paul Catholic Primary School, Lichfield

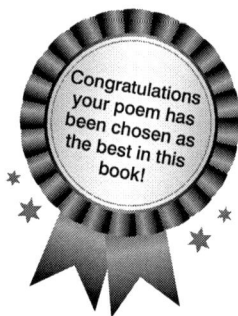

Congratulations your poem has been chosen as the best in this book!

My Magical Door

One day I went out for a walk,
And I had a little talk,
Guess who that talk was with?
My little friends and they are . . . fairies.
Here are some fairies I saw,
When I walked out my magical door
A bad fairy,
Who looked so hairy,
Robin Goodfellow,
He asked for a marshmallow,
And looked so yellow,
And I even saw a puck,
Who gave me good luck,
A naughty pixie,
Who tripped me up,
But then came a brownie,
Even more luck,
Then saw a Nikes,
Messing with the pikes,
Then I got lost,
But then came a will-o'-the-wisp,
Who guided me back home.

When I got home I saw
A small elf,
Sitting on a shelf,
And then I saw a shadow,
But it was just my daddy,
With a cup of Joe.

Kathrine Purchase (9)
SS Peter & Paul Catholic Primary School, Lichfield

Shopping With Mum

Every day after school
I sometimes wish
I could go to a pool.

But instead we have to shop,
My legs get tired,
I could sometimes drop.

My mum loves shopping
And it's not fair,
She is happy like a grizzly bear.

At the till she starts to talk,
My legs are aching,
I can barely walk.

Angelica Seidel (8)
SS Peter & Paul Catholic Primary School, Lichfield

A Space Dream

I had a dream the other night,
Where I was flying at such a height,
Suddenly a comet came whizzing past,
I tried to catch up, but I came last,
But I saw a star, and this was my chance,
If I moved quickly we could have a galaxy dance,
The comet had gone but I had not,
No way the comet said to me, 'That's your lot.'
The star and I then saw the sun,
With heat and light we could run and run,
So next time I dream of a comet shooting past,
The star and I will race it and not come last!

Francesca Maria Pegg (10)
SS Peter & Paul Catholic Primary School, Lichfield

Flowers

They blow through the sky,
Different types of them,
Different colours,
They're beautiful,
You see them often,
They are at shops,
You often give them to people.
What are they?

Megan Louise Price (10)
SS Peter & Paul Catholic Primary School, Lichfield

The Doctor

Master of the box
And the controller of clocks
Flying through time and space
And he is ace at it too
He has lots of friends
And spends lots of time with them on planets
And his name is The Doctor.

Alfie Johnson (10)
SS Peter & Paul Catholic Primary School, Lichfield

Cats Purr

Cats purr, cats drink milk,
They sit on your lap and sometimes they're fat.
They hate rats but not bats,
But sometimes they are lazy, even crazy.

Katie Agnieszka Syner (8)
SS Peter & Paul Catholic Primary School, Lichfield

Out Of This World

Standing on my blue gate,
I invited him in,

Six arms like a ladybird,
Two arms aren't normal,
Because they don't have hands,
Horns are for attack,
Four eyes on look-out, staring at me,

Teeth are needles for eating,
As wobbly as a jelly,
Knobbly as a line of buttons,
Bright and cheerful as a rainbow,
Daggers on his shoes,
Ears are tree branches,

Springs don't help the wobble,
As hairy as a dog,
Running in elf shoes,
Smells like fresh cut grass,
The moustache is for distraction,

Warm pizzas are his favourite,
Bang! When he falls on the slippery floor,
Sleeping under my bed for evermore,
Now he lives with me.

Emma Bartlett (10)
St Andrew's CE Primary School, Shrewsbury

My Alien!

Thorny and spiky from head to foot.
So sharp and spiky it can cut
Through a solid brick wall
And it can make Nesscliffe Hill fall.

As big as New York
But it likes to eat pork.
Thorny scales on his big fat body,
Smashing up lobbies and trolleys.

Behind my toy king
Was this alien thing.
He can go super big and super small,
Then sometimes he can go as round as a ball.

He has legs the size of a hamster
And a body the size of a little toy camper.
Sometimes he goes as big as a globe
But not as fat though.

Three days later he is gone,
Can't find him, he is gone, gone, gone,
Missing my alien friend,
Drives me round the bend.

Joseph Brammer (9)
St Andrew's CE Primary School, Shrewsbury

Out Of This World

The super speedy spaceship,
Raced through space,
Like a wild cheetah,
At a thunderous pace.

Whoosh! was the sound
As it raced towards the moon,
The astronauts are up in space,
They hope to see you soon.

Dani Staley (10)
St Andrew's CE Primary School, Shrewsbury

Out Of This World

Lurking behind a lamp post
Claws the size of knives
Spikes like teeth
A head like a giant banana
Long curvy French moustache poking out his nose
As skinny as a stick
Neck like a giraffe's or bigger
I invited him home for tea.

He didn't have many manners
Cuts up food with his claws
He saw curry in the fridge and ate it all
No more curry in the fridge.
Kept me awake last night
His moustache had curry sauce in it.

UFO in the sky
Like a plate that can fly.
Up the beam the alien went
He said to me, 'Xo curry!'
Never came back and I'm glad
It's all calm when the alien's not around.

Ben Ebrey (11)
St Andrew's CE Primary School, Shrewsbury

My Alien

Eating its veg,
I found Meg,
He mumbled,
'If I don't eat my veg, I'll lose my leg.'
Up till this day,
He's been grey,
Not pea green,
But soon he will be,
Right now he's a rainbow,
Meg is violet then blue,
Depends what mood,
Then he's blue,
He changes colour,
If you mention his brother,
Then he eats,
More greens,
And drinks,
With a lot of 'clinks'
Disappears back to space,
Comes back for another play.

Alisha King (11)
St Andrew's CE Primary School, Shrewsbury

The Alien

Wreeee! Wreeee!
From under my bed
Out he comes
His head is red
Standing three inches tall
I can hardly see him at all
An alien that is so immediately small
Legs like wind-blown strings
Such tiny things
My little best friend from above.

Charlie Thorpe (10)
St Andrew's CE Primary School, Shrewsbury

My Epic Alien

Eight eyes glared at me,
With happiness it ran to me.
Its six arms and four hands all wrapped round me.
He was tiny until I said all aliens were mean,
Then the prickles on his neck got bigger.
His neck got wider.
His prickles were skyscrapers.
And his neck was a tangled thorn bush.
But it was all just a trick.

We became friends, we played music
And I watched his telly.
I frightened him, he spooked me
Then we went where we met
It was my room.
We always started eating homework books.
But we had a fight
Then I chucked him in a bin lorry.
Then he got crushed like an orange in a juicer.

Harry Smith (10)
St Andrew's CE Primary School, Shrewsbury

My Alien Friend

Thump! Thump!
What was that
From my empty bare room?
Stamp! Stamp!
Who was that
From my empty bare room?

Hiding in my wardrobe
As slimy as Golden Syrup,
As squelchy as wet mud,
As stinky as my dad's socks,
It messed up my bedroom.

Morgan Nichole Cummins (10)
St Andrew's CE Primary School, Shrewsbury

Doughnut Bob

At the hot dog stand he was there,
With whiskers and curly ears like a cat,
Scaly and spotty, tangled up tail,
Blink, blink, six eyes it had,
Stomp, stomp, where did it go?

Finally I found him, took him home,
Ding, dong, who's at the door,
His friends were there,
Wanting to take him home.

Doughnut Bob was looking really low
Because I let him go,
But Doughnut Bob walks real slow,
He walks his dog round Tesco.

Nose and smile all happy and sweet,
As I watched him stomp off with his friends
I said, 'Bye-bye Doughnut Bob, hope to see you again.'

Bethany Roberts (10)
St Andrew's CE Primary School, Shrewsbury

My Pocket Friend

I first saw him at Nesscliffe Woods hibernating,
Small and sparkly eyes like Chihuahuas,
Kitten ears all slimy and scratchy,
Grinning like a clown.

Spots as big as ice bergs,
His body is a big leaf,
Ten pencil arms,
Spiderweb cracks.

Moles are gobstoppers,
Gills like long dangly hairs,
Sandals are whips,
My pocket friend.

Maddie Roberts (9)
St Andrew's CE Primary School, Shrewsbury

The Alien In The Parking Lot

In the car park jumped out an alien.
5.5 ft tall.
His fuzzy purple, pink and orange hair danced
Like a thousand snakes.
I could see right through his slimy green belly.
Believe me, it was not pretty.
He had two fangs.
Two rosy red cheeks.
Two brown legs.
A big blue nose.
A cap bright red.
A jacket so yellow.
His name was Beebles
From Planet Pickles.
His species was the Todac.
He may look different but he is just like you and me.
He could be friends with everybody.

Julia Ward (11)
St Andrew's CE Primary School, Shrewsbury

My Alien

Hiding in the corner of my room,
Cute and cuddly, eyes like a dog,
Gerbil ears all small and soft,
Smiling like a monkey,
Hair like a big black crazy fluffball.

Tall and slim,
Wobbly and curly,
As soft as a brown blanket,
Long and lanky,
Legs like an octopus,
Squirming like a worm,
I hope I'll see Greg again.

Molly Mewis (10)
St Andrew's CE Primary School, Shrewsbury

Stars

Burning bright
All through the night
Hot gases dance through the nuclear light
Supernova and Red Dwarf
As clear as the eye can see.
But I wonder how many trillion
Miles away they can actually be.

Yellow Dwarf, the biggest star,
It is visible in light,
It smoulders and heats the Earth
To everyone's delight.
Red, brown, orange, yellow,
White and blue,
Who knew the Milky Way could be
As colourful as you.

Emily Pauline Margaret Jaques (9)
St Andrew's CE Primary School, Shrewsbury

An Alien's Cloak

I first saw him in the woods
His disguise a cloak with a hood
Then he turned to look at me
At that moment I decided to flee

Next morning walking by the mere
I noticed something rather queer
A cloak in a tree
But there was something else I couldn't see
His flying saucer
Beneath the water
Suddenly it began to hover
Like a helicopter
Then it shot into the sky
So fast it was invisible to the bare eye.

Charlie Edward Benedict Henry (11)
St Andrew's CE Primary School, Shrewsbury

Out Of This World

It came hurtling out of space.
Then hit me in the face.
A great big fat alien,
Red with blue spots that join up like dots.
And it's as big as a fox.
His spaceship is a box.

His arms are like thin weedy twigs.
His eyes are as green as figs.
His head is as small as a pea.
He looks like he has sailed the sea.
Suddenly he makes a rumbling noise
Like laughing boys.

He runs off and hides.
But he tries to hide in some pies.
Then he flies
Out of this world.

Jack Todman (11)
St Andrew's CE Primary School, Shrewsbury

Doughnuts

Trembling in the pencil pot
The race of a rabbit
With four eyes
A doughnut middle
With wings
The feet of a bird staring at me.

It jumped into my pocket
And went to sleep
When it woke up it was blue!
Curiously I looked at it
It changed colour again.

I said, 'Go home.'
She turned as green as the greenest grass
And ran
Never seen again
Life was lonely after that.

Mia Jones (11)
St Andrew's CE Primary School, Shrewsbury

Slibobil

Soft and colourful skin, iridescent like a rainbow,
Eight runny noses, great sense of smell,
Ears as big as pears,
Three large eyes, one on his neck.

Thirty little arms, super, super cute,
A tummy like a doughnut,
So tempting to eat,
Different sized legs, really fast.

Met him in a hedge on Aston Way,
Slibobil is his name,
Do you know where he is?
Don't worry if you don't,
He might have been eaten by my other pet goat!

Mia Maddox (11)
St Andrew's CE Primary School, Shrewsbury

My Journey To Space!

Only a fleeting glimpse of the tall reflection of daylight,
There was no moon,
The sky was lit up,
Blazing stars gazing out of the night sky.

Millions of sparkles like diamonds,
The sky changed to orange, red and gold,
The night sky was lit up,
Gold, silver and bronze I could see.

I saw the sun, moon, Earth and many more.
Wake up, wake up,
I heard a voice,
Oh not again, I'm off, daydreaming,
What an adventure,
I hope more like that come!

Leanne Simone Mullett (9)
St Francis Xavier Catholic Primary School, Oldbury

The Forgotten Place

The asteroid belt has a face,
Especially as it has a place in space,
People who visit it get erased,
Because they get ferociously chased.

The orange, yellow sun,
Shoots balls of fire like a gun,
Mercury, Venus, Jupiter, Mars,
It floats around space past stars,
I'm alright at making space bars.

Mercury, Mercury,
The colour of Turkey,
Earth, Earth,
Where there is birth,
Venus, Venus,
That is quite far from Uranus.

Moon, moon,
We'll get there soon,
Mars, Mars,
Bigger than a vase.

Jupiter, Jupiter,
Wait . . . wait,
Let's take a break,
To watch this earthquake.

Neptune, Pluto,
The colour of blue,
Pluto, Pluto,
The only dwarf planet.
Sorry, sorry, but this is the end.

Romer Tayao (10)
St Francis Xavier Catholic Primary School, Oldbury

Off To The Sun We Go

Mercury, Venus,
Jupiter, Mars.
Bright sky light,
Throughout the stars.
From here I see the moon
Flying past, it soon flies
Off to the sun we go.

Nothing was loud,
But silent, no sound,
I loved the stars
Shooting around
Sun gleams
Stars beam
Fire burns
Planets turn
Day and night
Part with light
Darkness around
Rovers found
Off to the sun we go.

Last rays of sun
Shooting like a gun.
Air quivered with anticipation,
The sun had a lot of radiation,
Stretched around like a curtain above,
No one will see a flying dove.
The sun that burns, the star turns . . .
Now because my journey's over
Next time I will send a rover.

Cormac Jack Vance (10)
St Francis Xavier Catholic Primary School, Oldbury

Up To Darkness

5, 4, 3, 2,1,
I go, turn the engines on,
Mercury, Venus, Earth and Mars,
I'm going to see the stars!

Off we go into space,
I go and see Earth's face,
From the rocket to the moon,
I will get there very soon.

Travelling to the rocky red,
Just like everyone said,
Mountains here, mountains there,
They are not very rare.

Travelling through the asteroid belt,
All these asteroids will not melt,
Approaching Jupiter, asteroids everywhere,
Out in space, there's no air.

Rings of Saturn, just like they said,
All the people, including Edd,
Going to see all of this,
No one can raise their fist.

Travelling back to the green,
Remembering what I've seen,
Planets there in the sky,
Now to go and eat some pie.

Malachy Martin Tun (9)
St Francis Xavier Catholic Primary School, Oldbury

My Trip To Space!

I got in my rocket,
It was big and red,
I couldn't wait,
Was it all in my head?

Three, two, one, blast-off! I heard,
I was so excited,
Never had I been into space,
I felt so delighted!

I could see a planet
But I couldn't see which one,
Everything was black,
This was so much fun!

The rocket was so fast,
It seemed we were there so soon,
I think I know that planet,
Oh yeah, it was the moon!

I landed the rocket,
And fell on my knees,
I got up and walked out
And looked for moon cheese!

I got back in my rocket,
And made my way back home,
Oops, I forgot something,
Oh, it was my phone!

Molly Hannah Francis (10)
St Francis Xavier Catholic Primary School, Oldbury

The Solar System

The lit-up sky hidden by stars,
They turn and turn, don't worry they stay,
Like a candle, put out just by a blow,
As the stars shine they glow.

The sun, the sun is a big star, don't go away,
In a shape I always say,
As the planets go by they just sleep,
In the solar system I go, the rocket says beep, beep!

The planets that sleep and snore,
When we talk, they ignore,
When we stare they glare,
Although there are stars, there is no air!

Mars, Mars, Mars,
We can see stars,
Gazing up in the sky,
Having a stroll on you.

Pluto, Pluto, baby of them all,
You're not tall but you stall,
Up you are above the stars,
Can you hide because you're tiny?

Tapiwa Melissa Mavindidze (9)
St Francis Xavier Catholic Primary School, Oldbury

Out To Space

Slowly, slowly I shoot out to space
Looking at the Earth's round face
Finding all the shooting stars
To see if they are faster than racing cars.

Mercury, Mercury, are you hot
Or are you a small spot?
Mercury, Mercury, you are small
Mercury, when will you ever be tall?

Ilyas Hussain (10)
St Francis Xavier Catholic Primary School, Oldbury

125

The Shining Stars

Stars, stars burning bright,
In this dark and eerie night,
That give a lot of light,
At this tall height.

What would it be
To jump on the stars,
Yippee, yippee,
To jump on the stars.

The gleaming stars,
As golden as the sun,
Do not have anything,
To spin on.

They guide us through,
When we are lost,
The wise men used them,
At no cost.

But the main thing about stars
Is they are very far.

Martha Rose Lockett (9)
St Francis Xavier Catholic Primary School, Oldbury

Astronauts

A ir like a freezing cold giant ice cube
S tars glittering very shiny
T iny rocks floating in the air
R ockets going up to space
O ver the moon is the burning hot sun
N eptune is shiny blue
A stronauts floating in the air
U sually it is very cold on Neptune
T o take-off by counting down
S olar system is amazing.

Sophia Doreen Smith
St Francis Xavier Catholic Primary School, Oldbury

The Rocky Red Planet

The dawn's first ray of sunlight,
Gave me a fright,
I knew straight away,
That I had to go.

The rocky red planet,
Soon I landed on,
Gave me a fright without any light.

Mars is the planet,
Which went red with anger,
It was also very exciting.

We raced back home,
In our rocket,
I soon had my feet
On the soft pillow.

This was my chance,
To show my bits and bobs,
With amazement they patted me,
With glee on the back.

Simran Ria Jassi (9)
St Francis Xavier Catholic Primary School, Oldbury

Freezing Planets

The freezing planet crusted with ice
It makes me think of fluffy white rice.

Neptune has loads of ice
It looks like a bunch of frozen mice.

The ice is covered
With a blanket of snow.

There are no trees or fleas
That grow on Neptune.

Otuya Ugboh
St Francis Xavier Catholic Primary School, Oldbury

A Milky Way Day

The solar system dancing in my head,
Everyone else is dreaming in their bed,
While I am exploring up in space,
I might see the planet's face.

Mercury is an amazing place,
Its speed is an excellent pace,
Why don't you have a race?
What if I see a UFO with a person inside called Joe.

I will see all the stars,
I will see all the moons,
I will see Mars,
My snack will be prunes.

Mercury, Jupiter, Venus, Mars,
Up in the sky,
The twinkling stars,
All up high.

This was my Milky Way day.

Abigail Francis (9)
St Francis Xavier Catholic Primary School, Oldbury

Spaceship

S tarting countdown 3, 2, 1 . . . blast-off
P atiently riding up to the stars
A ll about up there exploring space
C alling aliens from the moon
E ach one has their own hole to rest
S tars of every kind twirling
H oping to see some swirling
 I hope to see them again
P assing by waving to them in the silver ship.

Bethany Cullen
St Francis Xavier Catholic Primary School, Oldbury

Jupiter, Earth, Venus And Mars

Jupiter, Earth, Venus and Mars,
I was floating above the stars,
In the dark sky of space,
I forgot to tie my lace.

Earth got small,
As round as a ball,
You cannot fall,
But it's not very tall.

Jupiter, what does it hold?
Nobody has been told,
The secrets still behold,
For the people who are bold.

Venus is as bright as a star,
It looks close but it's actually quite far,
Before you go, remember,
To take a Milky Bar.

Lewis Iezzi (10)
St Francis Xavier Catholic Primary School, Oldbury

Lunar Friends

L ike a robot in disguise
U ndercover like police
N ice like a starry night sky
A lways everlasting like God
R aging like a bull

F riendly like my teacher
R eally like me
I nvisible like God
E lf-like figures
N ormal like us
D aredevils like stunt me
S targazers like scientists!

Louis Woods
St Francis Xavier Catholic Primary School, Oldbury

Space Animation . . .

I finally leave my bright wonderful world,
To space I see, I twirl and curl,
Last rays of the sun on Earth,
The clouds like someone wanting to surf.

At last I arrive to see twinkling stars,
It looks like gold glitter just set in bars,
Black velvet sky is there,
I'd love to set a show for the mayor.

Suddenly I have a hesitation,
Then I see a space animation,
Planets spin round and round,
It makes me jump out of bounds.

It's finally time to go,
I'm heading down so low,
So bye-bye my space animation,
Now it's time for me to go back to my nation.

Kaleigh Truong (9)
St Francis Xavier Catholic Primary School, Oldbury

Lunar Friends

L ovely
U ltimate and do things awesomely
N ever land but
A lways quite ecstatic and joyful
R eally rare

F riendly around people
R eally king and keep the moon tidy
I ntelligent at physics
E verlasting
N ormal like us
D elightful
S uperb.

Dylan J
St Francis Xavier Catholic Primary School, Oldbury

Neptune, Mars And Stars

N eptune is so cold you could freeze!
E ven how bright is Neptune when it's blue?
P lanet Neptune is the most popular planet!
T he planet Neptune is made out of gas and water!
U niverse, Neptune is so blue your eyes turn blue.
N eptune is always famous because it's stayed for years
E ven though people don't go there anymore.

M ars is a bright orange planet
A nd it's a dusty planet!
R eally Mars is famous!
S ometimes Mars looks yellow!

S eems nights last longer if I see stars in the sky.
T hinking all the thoughts that I have on high!
A glimpse of shine makes me feel alive.
R are stars falls are burying me on fire.
S omeday, I want to be with all night.

Akolade Alabi (8)
St Francis Xavier Catholic Primary School, Oldbury

Discover Space

D aring mission
I lluminating world to pass
S tunning stars shining bright as we pass through the night
C omets passing by as quick as a flash
O nly ten minutes till we land
V ery excited
E veryone shouting
R eady to land

S olar system is as bright as can be
P ounding hearts from the
A stronauts, have we reached the land?
C ollecting samples to take back to Earth
E arth is just an inch away, can't wait to get back there today.

Christian O'Neil Faure (9)
St Francis Xavier Catholic Primary School, Oldbury

The Hottest Of Them All

Venus, are you really hot
Or are you as cold as a pot?
Off the Earth and into space,
Past the stars and past the planets,
And where we stuck to lots of magnets.

Going to Venus with lots of speed,
Approaching the planet in the lead,
Praying and hoping we lived to see,
The planet we were dreaming to be,
Swaying and dodging the rocks that came.

Day and night came and came,
As we landed where we dreamed to be,
Shooting stars flying past,
They must've been really fast,
The hottest planet of them all,
And now we know.

Codie Guest (10)
St Francis Xavier Catholic Primary School, Oldbury

The Solar System

The lovely bright stars
Shine dashingly in the night sky.
The moon shines brightly in the dark sky.
The mysterious secrets of Pluto.
They love the shining sun.
Pluto is as silver as a silver coin.
How bright is the sun.
Space is a lovely place.
You float like a boat in space.

The asteroid belt is a beautiful place.
The beautiful view of the planets
And the lovely view of space.

Kye Southall (9)
St Francis Xavier Catholic Primary School, Oldbury

Journey To Mars

J ourney to Mars
O ut of the world
U nder the world
R ed planet called Mars
N ever too late
E verlasting journey
Y ou would never believe the sights

T he vast space above us
O ut of the world we go

M ajor Max is never too late
A ir in his suit is going
R ed light flashing
S orry Major Max this is your time.

Macantony Tadiwanashe Guta (9)
St Francis Xavier Catholic Primary School, Oldbury

The Swirly Solar System

Slowly I walked into the huge rocket.
Then we would plunge to the huge planet.

I looked out the window,
I could see a shooting star.
It was faster than a racing car.

I looked out the window again,
And I could see a huge black hole,
It was bigger than a giant mole.

So now I am back on Earth,
From my trip to Saturn, Neptune and Mars,
So now I am back from all the stars.

Deleo Dhesi (9)
St Francis Xavier Catholic Primary School, Oldbury

Spaceship

S pectacular, shooting, soaring stars
P lummeting across the pitch-black sky
A nd an enormous sky
C rossing the moon
E normous spaceship
S tarry, smooth stars
H ilarious funny shaped planets
 I ncredible and outstanding spaceship
P itch-black in the starry sky.

Alisha Sandhu
St Francis Xavier Catholic Primary School, Oldbury

Spaceship

S oaring through the deep, dark, high sky
P arking my spaceship, I landed with a thump and a bump
A n alien hit me, I couldn't move
C arefully I opened the door, oooww!
'E xecute time!' the boss shouted
S lowly I backed away
'H urry!' an alien shouted. 'He's getting away.'
 I couldn't run anymore, they'd caught me
'P lease be our friend,' they shouted. 'Of course!' I answered.

Poppy H
St Francis Xavier Catholic Primary School, Oldbury

Spaceship

S oaring high up into the atmosphere
P lanets placed everywhere
A stronauts walking on the round, lumpy surface
C ompletely black
E xcept for
S himmering, shining stars
H otter than a blazing furnace
I nteresting, exciting, magnificent
P oisonous gases and no flowing water.

Shae Barnett (9)
St Francis Xavier Catholic Primary School, Oldbury

Sparkling Stars

Stars twinkling like diamonds in the sky
Making many sparkling shapes
Glowing brightly in the night sky
What an amazing sight

Shooting stars falling from the sky
Glowing like the sun
Shooting stars leaving a trail behind
What an amazing sight!

Mohammed Seraj (9)
St Francis Xavier Catholic Primary School, Oldbury

Lizzie The Launcher

R ocketing rockets flying away
O ver and over again they go in circles
C ountdown time is coming for Lizzie's multicoloured rocket
   to launch
K now that the rocket is launching in 3, 2, 1 . . .
E verything is perfectly fine until the meteors attack the rocket
T errified Lizzie screams in fear.

Fiona Eugene
St Francis Xavier Catholic Primary School, Oldbury

Galactus

G alaxy stars shooting by
A s I glide through the air no one is there
L ying in anti-gravity no one was mad at me
A ssuming the Silver Surfer will fly high
C hallenging mission I was on, no one knew I was gone
T alking about the last rushing rocket race
U sing oxygen to walk on the moon I found the Joker's goon
S tars are shiny bright like the sun.

Benjamin Avery
St Francis Xavier Catholic Primary School, Oldbury

Planets

P luto is large on the inside and small on the outside
L ittle as a ball
A stronauts ready to fly high
N ear in space in the sky
E arth is far away, never to be seen
T otally near to freezing Pluto
S tars, shooting, soaring across.

Grace Servando
St Francis Xavier Catholic Primary School, Oldbury

Pluto!

P eople argue this planet has vanished
L aunching on to Pluto would be freezing and frosty
U sing NASA people think Pluto is a dwarf planet
T o keep alive on Pluto you have to bounce and float on the
freezing frosty face of Pluto
O ther planets are triple the size of Pluto.

Bobbie-May Bradley (8)
St Francis Xavier Catholic Primary School, Oldbury

Lulu The Rocket

R evving rocket ready to take off
O pening the rocket doors to explore
C olourful is the rocket
K now how to fly the rocket
E ject the doors to get back down to Earth
T each the rocket how to fly on its own.

Rhianna Hurst
St Francis Xavier Catholic Primary School, Oldbury

Pluto!

P eople say it is a silver planet
L ife on Pluto is like an Oreo biscuit without the cream inside
U sing NASA people say Pluto has vanished like a balloon!
T he shining, silver stars are like silver balloons everywhere
O ther planets are not like the dwarf planet Pluto.

Junnat Naveed Chaudhry (9)
St Francis Xavier Catholic Primary School, Oldbury

137

Space!

S tars glittering up and up in the sky
P lanets are passing by
A stronaut floating high
C omets whizzing by
E xcited beyond belief.

Aidan Bedford
St Francis Xavier Catholic Primary School, Oldbury

Space

S ilent stars
P lanets playing
A stronauts jumping
C rumbling rocks
E arth, a long way away.

Mery Christina Falbi (9)
St Francis Xavier Catholic Primary School, Oldbury

Space!

S tarry vast world
P eople soaring in rockets
A rocket is rushing in the distance
C omets soaring everywhere
E arth is like a big blue ball.

Gurjeevan Singh
St Francis Xavier Catholic Primary School, Oldbury

Pluto

P luto is the most remote planet in the solar system
L ovely Pluto lights up the atmosphere
U nique and far, far away Pluto sits and waits for someone
T errific Pluto is cool as a cucumber
O ceanic atmosphere, easy on the eye.

Faithann Snow
St Francis Xavier Catholic Primary School, Oldbury

Space

S hooting stars through the sky
P ounding with fear in the air
A stronaut missing family
C ertain signs of adventure
E arth is like a big blue ball.

Grace Connell
St Francis Xavier Catholic Primary School, Oldbury

Space!

S pace is safe, starry and spacious
P eace is in space and you can fly
A breathtaking place and really vast
C atching breath so you can't breathe
E arth is like a blue, big ball in space.

Joshua F
St Francis Xavier Catholic Primary School, Oldbury

Earth And Mars

E veryone lives on Earth except aliens
A liens live on all planets but Earth
R ockets zoom way up high in outer space
T he moon brightens up the night sky
H ow many planets?

A stronauts on the moon
N eptune, moon, Earth, Mars, Saturn, what else?
D ark night sky

M any planets except Pluto are in space
A n alien is green
R abbits on the moon?
S tars, stars, wonderful stars and planets!

Amy Louise O'Neill (9)
St Michael's CE Primary School, Birmingham

Car/home

C lean and shiny
A mazing when you buy one
R enault the coolest car you've ever seen

H ard and strong
O ld and rotten
M ine to live in
E ager to buy.

Ethan Green (8)
St Michael's CE Primary School, Birmingham

Out Of This World

Out in space
Amongst the world
What's out there?
Let's find out.

There could be
Winter World
Spring World
Summer World
Autumn World.

Out in space
Amongst the world
What's out there?
Let's find out.

There could be
Candy World
Vegetable World
Fruit World
Greedy World.

Out in space
Amongst the world
What's out there?
Let's find out.

There could be
Random World
Metal World
Sponge World
But our world is still here!

Ella Hay (9)
St Michael's CE Primary School, Birmingham

Reverse Universe

It's a full moon, midnight, I'm in my bed,
Can't get to sleep, no thoughts in my head.
Waiting for the Sandman with his golden dust,
I must get to sleep, I must, I must, I must!
I start to drift, my eyes grow weak.
Fidgeting, crying, I hear a creak.
I open one eye, then the other,
Feeling scared, I want my mother.
I scramble onto the cold, hard floor,
Feeling unsure, I open the door,
Like someone has pushed me, I fall to the ground,
This is a strange, new world I have found!

The people have wheels, the cars have legs,
They have eyes on their feet and toes on their heads,
From a green grass sky, flowers hang down,
I tiptoe through fluffy clouds on the ground,
Purring dogs run from barking cats,
A piper is following flute playing rats,
I don't belong in this reverse universe.
I don't want to be here, is this a curse?
Through a puddle of socks, I find a plain, dull door,
Is this the door I came through before?
I turn the handle and to my surprise
I'm back in my bedroom, with open eyes,
Everything is normal . . . or so it seems . . .
Far away, a cat barks . . . was it really just a dream?

Stella Haden (9)
St Michael's CE Primary School, Birmingham

Out Of This World

O n the spaceship on the way there
U ncomfortable in bed
T he view is amazing

O bviously missing my family
F rom the first day I came, I always wanted to have a party

T his is the person that wants to discover life in space
H ere is a picture that I took of the Earth
 I t's an amazing experience
S o, I really do miss home

W ow! The Earth looks so small
O n the way back I might cry
R ight . . . let's go home
L oved my time in space
D inner time! I missed Earth food.

Faye Brinkworth (10)
St Michael's CE Primary School, Birmingham

Out Of This World

O uter space wonders
U p in the starry skies
T otally amazing

O pen to adventures
F riendly aliens

T o be investigated more
H appy as can be
 I s there anybody out there?
S parkling like glitter

W onders from out of this world
O ohing and ahhing at the sights
R eady to explore
L ovely memories
D own, back to Earth.

Laura Gray (11)
St Michael's CE Primary School, Birmingham

The Galaxy

Let's go in a rocket
Just you and me
Let's explore the galaxy.

If we look up
To the sky we will pass
White fluffy clouds
Way up high.

What will we see
Just you and me
Riding around the galaxy?

The galaxy is massive
It's beautiful and bright
I'm so glad we went out tonight.

Jessica Baker (8)
St Michael's CE Primary School, Birmingham

Rocket Aliens

R aces into the sky with a bang
O ver hills and mountains, and that is tall
C an go anywhere you like in the universe
K *aboom* . . . as the rocket takes off
E ating in the rocket as it floats around
T akes a lot of steam with it

A lways stay away from aliens, as they're so disgusting
L eaves a trail of slimy goo
 I n space forever because nobody likes them
E ating weird stuff, like mushy peas
N ever go back down because they're scared of humans
S tays on the moon as they like to float around.

Emily Douglas (8)
St Michael's CE Primary School, Birmingham

Monster World

Monster World is so, so scary,
With vampires and ghosts and something hairy.
All your fears will appear right there,
Even a shark or a big, bad bear.
So who lives here in this scary world?
Something big, bad, gruesome and wild,
Werewolves howl all night through
And you always think they're out to get you
With their yellow eyes and scary teeth
And Yetis with big hands and big feet.
These gruesome creatures are all in the sky,
They are all above us and are very, very high!

Abigail Nicholls-Hall (9)
St Michael's CE Primary School, Birmingham

I Have A Passion For Dance

I have a passion for dance,
I also like to prance
Around the room.
Mum says to control it but that's my doom.
I don't just dance for a bit
I dance four days a week.
So, I guess I can say I dance till I'm weak.
I don't just have a passion for dance
I have a passion for modern, gymnastics, ballet and tap.
After I dance I always get a tap on the back,
Oh, not forgetting the gigantic clap.

Aliyah Miles (10)
St Michael's CE Primary School, Birmingham

Space

S tars twinkling in the sky at night,
   They look so lovely and bright.
P lanets of different shapes and sizes,
   They bring lots of surprises.
A stronauts landing on the moon,
   They'll be back soon.
C raters big and bumpy,
   Like a block of cheese that's lumpy.
E arth spinning around
   Without making a sound.

Mia Irving (10)
St Michael's CE Primary School, Birmingham

Candyworld

Candyworld awesome and sweet
Very tasty indeed!
All the planets made out of candy get eaten up by me.
Milky stars glowing bright get melted by the hot, candy sun.

On Earth cars race past the chocolate walls of a great castle,
Everyone rattles to see the fantastic Gummy Bears.
Then everyone looks up to see Uranus glowing
Like bright blue bubblegum.

Eniola Gabriel (7)
St Michael's CE Primary School, Birmingham

Homework

H elping my teachers in school
O utside with my friends
M aking cakes with my family
E ating the cakes with my family
W orking hard in class
O ut with my family
R eading books at home
K ing and queen live happy ever after.

Chelsea Smith (11)
St Michael's CE Primary School, Birmingham

Out Of This World

Standing in front of me in a glass so tall,
I wonder to myself, *will I eat it all?*
So many delights on top of each other,
I'm not sharing this with my little brother.
Fruit, jelly, chocolate, ice cream,
I pinch myself, is this a dream?
This tower of treats all for me,
You're out of this world knickerbocker glory!

Lily-Mae Adkins (8)
St Michael's CE Primary School, Birmingham

All About Me

I go to school, St Michael's the name,
The teachers are cool and they all know my name.

Sometimes I'm good and sometimes I'm bad,
I know how much this makes my mum and dad mad.

I love my sport but footie is my game,
Come on you Baggies, I hope the boys win today.

James Stephen Bonning (7)
St Michael's CE Primary School, Birmingham

My Pet Dog, Rosie!

R idiculously fast
O bedient
S illy
I ntelligent
E veryone's friend.

We love her!

Deacon Jones (10)
St Michael's CE Primary School, Birmingham

Friend

F riends are the best
R easons to not complain
I mportant friends matter
E mergencies matter the most
N eeding help and we will be there
D oing what matters to you makes me happy.

Alease Wheeler (10)
St Michael's CE Primary School, Birmingham

School

S erious teachers try to make
C hildren clever and
H appy
O h be good
O h be good
L earning can be fun!

Samantha Greenhill (8)
St Michael's CE Primary School, Birmingham

School

S chool is the best
C lass teacher is lovely
H ow lovely is it not to be at home
O h how lovely school is
O nly five teachers in the classroom
L ovely and kind people in class.

Elissia Bolt (10)
St Michael's CE Primary School, Birmingham

Winter Forest

W inter is as cold as ice
I cicles hang down
N ature is hibernating
T he heating's on full blast
E veryone wraps up warm
R unning in the snow.

Mia Lily Watkins (7)
St Michael's CE Primary School, Birmingham

Space

S tart the shuttle we're going now
P acked lunch with chicken sandwich, yay!
A lert, alert a comet coming
C oming back to Earth yay!
E veryone, I'm home, I'm glad to be back.

Toni Mercy Adebayo (8)
St Michael's CE Primary School, Birmingham

Candy

C is for candy cane
A is for Aeros
N is for nice
D is for double mint gums
Y is for York peppermint pattie.

Alisha Shahid (7)
St Michael's CE Primary School, Birmingham

Bunny

B ouncing bunny
U pside down
N aughty bunny hopping around
N ice bunny sitting down
Y ou're up late, get to town.

Bethany Robertson (9)
St Michael's CE Primary School, Birmingham

May

M igration is over, everyone is coming back
A maryllises booming everywhere I look
Y elling with pleasure as I run through meadows.

Caelyn Wilbanks (9)
St Michael's CE Primary School, Birmingham

YOUNG WRITERS
INFORMATION

We hope you have enjoyed reading this book –
and that you will continue to in the coming years.

If you're a young writer who enjoys reading and
creative writing, or the parent of an enthusiastic poet or
story writer, do visit our website
www.youngwriters.co.uk. Here you will find free
competitions, workshops and games, as well as
recommended reads, a poetry glossary and our blog.

If you would like to order further copies of
this book, or any of our other titles give us
a call or visit **www.youngwriters.co.uk.**

Young Writers
Remus House
Coltsfoot Drive
Peterborough
PE2 9BF

(01733) 890066 / 898110
info@youngwriters.co.uk